Building Social Awareness in **Autistic Children** and their **Peers Using Minecraft®**

by the same author

A Therapist's Guide to Neurodiversity Affirming Practice with Children and Young People
Raelene Dundon
ISBN 978 1 83997 585 1
eISBN 978 1 83997 586 8

Talking with Your Child about Their Autism Diagnosis
A Guide for Parents
Raelene Dundon
ISBN 978 1 78592 277 0
eISBN 978 1 78450 577 6

The Parents' Guide to Managing Anxiety in Children with Autism
Raelene Dundon
ISBN 978 1 78592 655 6
eISBN 978 1 78592 657 0

PDA in the Therapy Room
A Clinician's Guide to Working with Children with Pathological Demand Avoidance
Raelene Dundon
ISBN 978 1 78775 347 1
eISBN 978 1 78775 348 8

Building Social Awareness in Autistic Children and their Peers Using Minecraft®

A Step by Step Guide to Running Neurodiversity-Affirming Groups

Raelene Dundon

Original Illustrations by Chloe-Amber Scott and Jessica Scott

Jessica Kingsley Publishers
London and Philadelphia

First published in Great Britain in 2026 by Jessica Kingsley Publishers
An imprint of John Murray Press

2

Front cover image source: Chloe-Amber Scott and Jessica Scott

A CIP catalogue record for this title is available from the British Library and the Library of Congress

ISBN 978 1 80501 853 7
eISBN 978 1 80501 854 4

Printed and bound in the United States by Integrated Books International

Jessica Kingsley Publishers' policy is to use papers that are natural, renewable and recyclable products and made from wood grown in sustainable forests. The logging and manufacturing processes are expected to conform to the environmental regulations of the country of origin.

Jessica Kingsley Publishers
Carmelite House
50 Victoria Embankment
London EC4Y 0DZ

www.jkp.com

John Murray Press
Part of Hodder & Stoughton Limited
An Hachette UK Company

The authorised representative in the EEA is Hachette Ireland,
8 Castlecourt Centre, Dublin 15, D15 XTP3, Ireland (email: info@hbgi.ie)

For Andrew

Contents

Acknowledgements

Thank you again to my amazing husband and best friend, Andrew Tompkins, for your support, guidance and encouragement. I could not have completed this book without you.

Thank you also to my talented illustrators, Chloe-Amber Scott and Jessica Scott, who have brought my vision for this book to life with their wonderful images.

A special thank you to Sarah and her gorgeous girls, who originally introduced me to Minecraft® and planted the seed of an idea to use the game as a theme for a social skills curriculum. Your insights and experiences have continued to guide me in becoming a better therapist and advocate.

Thank you to my neurodivergent colleagues, who have enlightened and supported me to explore and embrace neurodiversity-affirming practice so I can keep learning and growing with my clients and advocating for their rights and needs while celebrating their uniqueness.

Finally, thank you to all the children and families that have been involved in our social groups over many years. Your enthusiasm for our programs and willingness to grow with us has confirmed the power in creating a safe and accepting space for young people, and encouraged me to write this second edition to provide the opportunity for many more children to learn about accepting and celebrating difference in a fun and engaging way.

Introduction

This second edition of my Minecraft® Social Skills Curriculum represents a significant shift for me personally and professionally in the way that I approach supporting all young people, but especially autistic children, with their social-emotional development. In particular, I have been influenced by the rise of neurodiversity-affirming practice, which has really brought into the spotlight the fact that we need to be accepting and accommodating of difference, and that we can provide support to all children to recognize and understand others and show compassion and empathy to those that are different from ourselves.

Since the first edition was released in 2019, my understanding and passion for neurodiversity-affirming practice has grown, and with it a clearer vision regarding the rights of all neurotypes, and recognition that we should embrace the unique social and communication styles of autistic individuals rather than trying to change them. In late 2019, after many years of wondering, I found myself going through the assessment process to be formally diagnosed as autistic and ADHD. This was really the end of one journey of realization and discovery, and the beginning of another as an autistic individual, autistic parent and autistic professional. It was also an opportunity to begin the process of reviewing my experience through the lens of neurodivergence, which has made a huge difference in my understanding of myself and also enhanced my understanding of my clients (as a psychologist and play therapist).

Something that I have always firmly believed in is the idea that it shouldn't just be the responsibility of autistic individuals to make changes to meet the needs of neurotypical individuals. However, on reviewing the first edition of this book in a new light, it became clear that it was largely focused on supporting autistic children to understand neurotypical social skills rather than building confidence in their own social abilities. What we know now is that programs that focus on teaching autistic individuals to socialize in neurotypical ways tend to promote masking. They also send the misguided message to autistic children that the way they socialize and communicate is inherently wrong and needs to be corrected. That was certainly not my intention in creating my program and is something that I am grateful to now have the opportunity to correct in this edition.

My aim with this second edition was to create a program that not only supports autistic individuals to build confidence in their skills and awareness of themselves, but also to support their peers, both neurotypical and neurodivergent, to understand each other better. Consequently, the main premise of this new edition is to promote acceptance and understanding of difference. I hope that by providing opportunities for discussion around what it looks like to communicate in different ways and what it looks like to be social in different ways, we can promote understanding that there is not one right way to engage and connect with others.

Ultimately, I want to support all children to recognize that differences make them unique and interesting, and that they can accept their peers, autistic or not, for who they are rather than expecting them to change to fit in. If we learn to be more accepting and curious about the differences between us, we can develop a better understanding of ourselves and others and all seek to bridge gaps that arise in communication to find shared meaning and experience. The Double Empathy Problem, a concept which I talk about in Chapter 2, really illustrates this fact beautifully in recognizing that the miscommunication and awkwardness that is often reported when autistic and neurotypical individuals socialize together is actually the result of autistic individuals having difficulty understanding things from a neurotypical perspective and neurotypical individuals having difficulty understanding things from an autistic perspective. Rather than these challenges being a "one-way street" and the responsibility of the autistic individual to fix them, there is now recognition that we all need to be more aware and accepting in accommodating the differences of the individuals around us so that we are all able to communicate effectively and feel understood.

This new program will provide you with the resources that you need to be able to run groups in a way that is inclusive of all children and that really promotes the idea of acceptance through a medium that is relevant to all children, not just those that identify as autistic. Minecraft® is a very popular game, and I think that part of the magic of this group program is that it has been able to be built around something that is so universally loved and that really does appeal to children of all ages, all cultures, and certainly all neurotypes.

My hope is that those of you who used the first version of this social program will embrace the changes that I have made, and see the new material as being a positive shift to supporting all children to build their confidence, their social awareness, their self-worth and their understanding of themselves and others. And if you are new to the program, I am excited to share a more neurodiversity-affirming approach to supporting social development in the children that you support.

So, please embrace the neurodiversity-affirming direction that the program has taken, and once again – happy Minecrafting!

PART 1
Social Awareness and Minecraft®

CHAPTER 1

What Are Social Skills?

Social skills can be described as the collection of abilities required to engage, interact and communicate with others in both verbal and nonverbal ways within a particular context. They are skills that we use every day when we are around other people to tune in to how others are feeling and what they might be thinking, predict what others may do in different situations, express our wants and needs, respond to the wants and needs of others, and continually review and adapt our behavior to meet the challenge of ever-changing social landscapes and societal expectations.

Social development in humans is complex and has been found to be influenced by a variety of factors including biology, environment and culture. With genes and brain development setting the stage in utero, social skills develop from birth and continue to evolve throughout childhood and adolescence, and into adulthood.

According to our current understanding of typical developmental stages, infants learn through interactions with carers and the environment that vocalizations, expressions of emotion and gestures have meaning. As they grow, children then start to show interest in peers and become more proficient in communicating their needs and seeking out interactions. But it is not until around the age of five years that children develop an understanding that they have different thoughts, feelings and beliefs to other people.

In the early school years, children learn about themselves as individual beings and seek out social connections with peers to feel like they belong. These early years of school provide opportunities for understanding and forming friendships, managing conflict with peers, developing communication skills and learning to regulate emotions.

Moving into adolescence, further social development occurs, as the connections with peers become more complex.

Adolescents develop a sense of identity by relating to those in their social circles and build a stronger sense of their thoughts and beliefs which have a greater influence on their choices and behavior. Through previous experiences and knowledge gained from others, adolescents also build skills in adapting to changing social situations, establishing stronger and deeper relationships with others, and altering behavior according to where they are and who they are with.

Finally, adults experience further social development and maturity which supports them to understand and navigate the complexities of intimate relationships, manage the different expectations and personalities in the workplace, maintain friendships and family connections, and operate effectively in a world reliant on social interaction to ensure they have everything they need to live.

With the dynamic nature of social interactions, and the ever-changing social landscape that we live in, it may be that our social skills never stop developing. Given that we use these skills every day, and throughout our lives, it is not surprising that gaining a better understanding of how social skills develop and why we need them has become the focus of many clinicians and theorists. One way we can make sense of social skills is to consider them as being made up of two connected elements: social awareness and social behavior.

SOCIAL AWARENESS

When we talk about social awareness, we are talking about a collection of abilities that allow us to understand emotions in ourselves and others, feel empathy and respond to others in need, see other people's perspectives, and recognize and be accepting of diversity among people and cultures. Social awareness can be thought of as a system involving mostly internal processes such as our thoughts, feelings and knowledge about ourselves and others, and includes qualities or abilities such as self-awareness and self-regulation, empathy, perspective taking and social problem solving.

Self-awareness

While being able to understand the communication, feelings and experiences of others is certainly important in our social interactions, to understand others we need to first have a clear and deep understanding of ourselves. We need to be aware of our wants and needs, our likes and dislikes, our strengths and challenges and our values and beliefs to be able to effectively navigate social situations, predict our own responses, implement coping strategies when needed and seek out social interactions and connections that sustain us and help us grow. Developing self-awareness and insight is a lifelong process that starts in early childhood and can be nurtured by having opportunities to think, feel and reflect on our experiences from a young age.

Self-regulation

Another essential aspect of social interaction is the ability to effectively manage our own emotions and behavior, particularly in response to others, which is often referred to as self-regulation. To do this we need to be able to recognize and understand our own emotions, manage our reactions to people or situations that elicit strong feelings, understand how our behavior impacts others, and have knowledge about what behavior is generally expected in different settings and in response to different social scenarios. In children, opportunities for co-regulation with a supportive adult at times of intense emotion form the basis of what will eventually be self-regulation; however, this takes considerable time. While children typically begin to build skills in self-regulation at around the age of three or four years, they continue to require support from others to regulate as they grow, with self-regulation abilities continuing to develop into adulthood.

Empathy

Empathy can be described as the ability to recognize and relate to the feelings, thoughts and experiences of others. It involves being able to identify how someone might be feeling in a particular situation and seeking to understand their perspective by drawing on similar experiences in our own lives. Empathy can help us to predict the actions of others in social situations and allows us to connect with others and demonstrate understanding and care, which is at the heart of all positive social relationships.

Social communication (receptive)

At the core of being social is communicating with others and, to have positive interactions, individuals must be able to understand the communication of others. In even the most basic interaction with another person, we are taking in and interpreting social communication cues such as the other person's facial expressions, body language, and any words or signs they may be using. In that same moment we may also be considering previous interactions we have had with that person, the context of the current interaction, and the message we want to convey in response. Our understanding of the situation and the communication of others helps to guide our responses.

Perspective taking

Perspective taking or the ability to see things from another person's perspective is sometimes referred to as "putting yourself in someone else's shoes," and as you can imagine, is at the core of many aspects of social interaction. When an individual has well-developed perspective taking ability, they are able to consider how others may experience a situation and recognize that that experience may be different to their own. This can help us predict how others may respond to our words and behavior, and can impact on how we interact with the people we are with and the environment we are in. While we are not usually conscious of it, we use perspective taking all the time to understand other people's emotions and behavior, and to guide our own words and actions.

Social problem solving

It seems to be the nature of interacting with people that there will be times when, either within our social interactions or due to the environment we are in, unexpected or unpredictable things happen. At these times, we need to use our social problem solving skills to find ways to manage situations effectively. We do this by being flexible in our thinking, considering possible scenarios and outcomes, understanding other people's points of view and compromising. These skills require the use of imagination as a tool to facilitate our ability to be adaptable and flexible, and to look at situations from different perspectives to find effective solutions.

SOCIAL BEHAVIOR

If we consider social awareness to be a collection of our internal social processes, social behavior can be thought of as the external expression of those processes that enables interaction with others. Social behavior is what we do in social situations to share our thoughts, feelings and knowledge and to respond to the people and environment we interact with. Social behaviors can include social communication, listening, cooperation, assertiveness and how we form friendships.

Social communication (expressive)

As we have already discussed, there is a lot to consider when we are processing and interpreting the communication of others, but there are also a lot of factors that impact how we express ourselves. Communication with others can take many forms. We may use verbal speech, which can include the words we use but also tone and volume. We may use signs or the written word. Nonverbal communication, such as facial expressions and body language, also conveys a message to our social partner in an interaction. We can use all these communication tools to express our thoughts, feelings, wants and needs to others, and these ways of communicating are all equally valid and important.

Listening

When others communicate with us in social situations, they usually rely on us to listen to what they are choosing to express and to show our understanding. While the processing of information may not be an external behavior, the way that we listen can communicate a message to our communication partner. We may use our own social tools such as facial expressions and body language to express our level of interest and communicate our understanding, all while processing and formulating a response.

Cooperation

Whenever we work or play with others, at preschool, school, home or in the community, we need abilities that enable us to cooperate to achieve a goal or follow a plan. To cooperate effectively we need to be able to tolerate the presence of others in our environment, give and receive help, lead and follow, compromise, and work together. These skills also involve the ability to pay attention to the people we are with and what is happening around us, so we can actively adapt what we are doing to suit the situation and what is needed to achieve a desired outcome.

Assertiveness

We mentioned the importance of self-awareness earlier, but it is not enough to just know ourselves well –we also require the skills to effectively advocate for our own needs and stand up for what we believe in. This is often referred to as being assertive. To be assertive, we need to first recognize that our wants and needs are important and that our voice has value. We then need to feel confident to speak up and be able to communicate in a way that is likely to be well understood by others (even if they don't agree). This is a skill that is essential in all relationships—friendships, classmates, work colleagues, intimate partnerships, commercial transactions—to ensure we are able to share ideas and opinions, voice our concerns, and communicate our needs.

Forming friendships

The ability to make and maintain friendships is often seen as the ultimate social goal. Friendship is not just about interaction; it is about making a meaningful connection with another person that lasts across time. Although friendships can look very different for all of us, to form successful friendships we generally need many of the social skills already mentioned, including being able to see others' perspectives, empathy, social communication skills, self-awareness, self-regulation and problem-solving skills. In addition, friendships involve shared experience, enjoyment, care and support that is reciprocal in nature. Having friends and experiencing a feeling of belonging is often viewed as essential to wellbeing and has been well documented as being a protective factor against the adverse effects of mental health disorders and social isolation.

SOCIAL SKILLS IN CONTEXT

Although the importance of social skills is well established, it can be easy to forget that the way we seek out social connection, and our ideas and understanding about which social behaviors are most desirable and acceptable, depend on many factors and are not universally defined.

How are social skills influenced by biology and experience?

An individual's personal qualities, which are formed through both biology and experience, will influence how that person engages in social interaction.

We are born with inherited personality traits, often described as our temperament, which are determined by genetics and are thought to form the foundation of our emotional and physical responses to life events. In particular, emotional reactivity and arousal regulation, often linked to the stress response, will influence how an individual engages with and responds to others in social situations.

The environment we are brought up in and our social experiences from infancy then interact with these traits to shape our personality development. For example, the responsiveness of parents and carers to our early social overtures, and positive and negative social experiences as we grow, further influence our social behaviors in different settings.

Ultimately, whether particular personal qualities are valued or not often depends on a society's dominant culture and preferred social behaviors.

How does culture impact on social skills?

The culture in which we live our lives has a big influence on the social rules that we are expected to follow in society, and consequently the social skills that are most valued.

When we think about culture, we often focus on the influence of an individual's ethnicity or religion; however, culture can encompass the beliefs, values, rituals and practices of any group of people. Accordingly, culture can be discussed in broad terms around large groups and whole populations (e.g. "Western culture") or in much more nuanced ways (e.g. "LGBTQI+ culture" or "family culture").

In modern society, what are generally considered acceptable social behaviors tend to be driven by the majority and are often associated with past traditions or beliefs that may or may not still be a part of current thinking. Social skills therefore tend to be linked to whatever is currently seen as polite, good manners or respectful within a particular population and can actually vary quite widely within and between cultures. This variation can lead to miscommunication and confusion when there are different social rules or acceptable social behaviors within a culture, as well as between cultures, during social interaction.

For example, one social situation that attracts many differing ideas of appropriate social behaviors across cultures is mealtimes. Some cultures see eating with your hands as most appropriate; others place importance on using cutlery. In some cultures, belching or burping after a meal is considered a sign of respect to the cook as it indicates satisfaction and a full stomach. However, belching in front of others is considered rude and a breach of social rules in places like the UK and Australia. It all depends on where you are and who you are with.

Considering current culture in Western countries in a broad sense, "good" social skills often include behaviors such as greetings, saying "please" and "thank you," and making eye contact. It is also considered acceptable to display moderate levels of emotion in public (e.g. sadness, disappointment, excitement, etc.). In contrast, some cultures around the world consider making eye contact disrespectful and speaking to someone from a higher class or position is not appropriate unless they have initiated an interaction first. It may also be considered inappropriate to display emotion in public settings. While we may find differences across cultures puzzling at times and perhaps see our own social rules as making the most sense, the reality is that there is no one right way to socialize, and we are all influenced by the social conventions within which we have grown and lived.

While it is important to be aware of cultural norms and expectations regarding social skills and to consider what is preferred within the culture in which we live, we also need to be more accepting and understanding of individual differences in social expression rather than seeing the way any one culture operates as the only acceptable way to socialize. Looking at social skills from a neurodiversity-affirming perspective is a positive way to support all children to do this.

CHAPTER 2

How Does a Neurodiversity-Affirming Approach Change the Way We Think about Social Skills?

The concept of neurodiversity has been around formally since the 1990s and encompasses the idea that there is natural diversity among human brains in the population. Working with this idea, the neurodiversity-affirming paradigm suggests that while there may be a majority of individuals whose brains work in a way that is considered the norm (referred to as neurotypical), individuals with brains that function differently from the majority (referred to as neurodivergent) are equally important within society, and do not need to be fixed or cured.

But what does this have to do with social skills? Well, for individuals with neurodivergent brains, such as children and adults who are autistic, ADHD or have learning disabilities, their social abilities have historically been labelled as "impaired" or "deficient" and in need of intervention. For example, the official diagnostic criteria for autism in the DSM-5 (an official diagnostic manual used to identify psychiatric and developmental disorders in which autism is currently included) lists impairments in social communication, understanding and relationships as key features. Consequently, the focus of supports and therapy for autistic children has often been to fix these apparent deficits by teaching them "appropriate" social skills, which are those used by the majority of people in their society.

More recently, however, we have seen the discussion about the social skills of autistic individuals, and those with other neurodivergent neurotypes, starting to change in line with neurodiversity-affirming principles. These principles are based around human rights and focus on the need to presume competence, promote autonomy, accept all communication styles, listen to those with lived experience, and tailor supports to individual needs. While these principles should apply to all people, they are especially important for people with disability, including the autistic community, because they have historically been treated as less capable and had less say in how they live their lives.

Changes to the way we view social skills have been driven by the emergence of concepts such as the "Double Empathy Problem," a better understanding of masking and the potential damage it can cause, and the introduction of autistic culture as a way to explain social differences.

We will explore each of these ideas in more detail below, but first, let's review what we know about autism.

WHAT IS AUTISM?

From a neurodiversity-affirming perceptive, autism can be described as a neurotype characterized by unique social and communication styles and preferences for routine and predictability that can also be associated with intense sensory sensitivities and preferences, stimming, and passionate interests. While diagnostic manuals continue to refer to autism as a developmental disorder, many members of the autistic community and their allies recognize that although autistic features can be disabling, autistic individuals are not disordered or broken, but are a natural variation among human beings.

It is also important to note that autistic individuals can have a combined neurotype with other neurodivergences such as intellectual disability, attention deficit hyperactivity disorder and learning disability, which can impact on their presenting features and support needs.

THE DOUBLE EMPATHY PROBLEM

The Double Empathy Problem, as proposed by autistic researcher Damian Milton, suggests that rather than autistic individuals having a deficit in social abilities, there is a mutual disconnect and lack of reciprocal understanding between autistic and neurotypical individuals when engaged in social interactions. In other words, while it may be difficult for autistic individuals to understand neurotypical experience and social conventions, it is also difficult for neurotypical individuals to understand and empathize with autistic experience, and that is why social challenges occur between them. This shifts the focus from attributing social challenges solely to the autistic individual, to recognizing that social interaction is two-way and both parties have a responsibility for its success.

Recent research supports this idea, with studies finding that when two autistic or two neurotypical individuals interact, social challenges are not obvious. However, when autistic and neurotypical individuals interact together, there is a social awkwardness or disconnection in the interaction that is evident to observers.

While originally discussed in relation to autistic individuals in social situations, I believe the Double Empathy Problem is relevant to any individuals who socialize in ways that are different from the norm. Holding this idea in mind when discussing social skills provides recognition of the need for all children to learn about diverse social styles and develop understanding and acceptance of anyone who is different to themselves.

MASKING

Masking is the term often used to describe the act of hiding your true self or parts of yourself to achieve greater social acceptance or to "fit in." Sometimes referred to as "social camouflaging," it is a strategy that may be used consciously or unconsciously by individuals to hide their neurodivergent traits and ultimately appear more neurotypical at school, at work or in the community. For example, an individual may suppress a stimming behavior, exaggerate facial expressions to mirror those of peers, or pretend to enjoy a social situation (that is internally causing distress) to gain peer acceptance or avoid exclusion.

While it is sometimes argued that everyone masks at times, such as having a professional persona that may be more reserved than how we are with friends, masking for neurodivergent individuals comes with considerably higher costs. The difference for neurodivergent individuals is that they are often forced to hide their natural way of being, their true selves, and put aside their internal needs and wants, in order to be accepted. And learning, often from a very young age, that your true self is not acceptable to others, that you must pretend to be someone else to be liked and included, and that your needs are not important, can have significant negative consequences for their mental health. Unfortunately, traditional social skills programs have tended to promote masking by teaching that using neurotypical social skills is the only acceptable way to socialize.

Taking a neurodiversity-affirming approach to social skills means recognizing that just like there is natural variation in brain types, there is natural variation in the ways that individuals socialize. Rather than teaching individuals that there is only one way to engage in social interactions, we need to support children to understand their own social style as well as the styles of others, and to be accepting of difference. Recognizing and normalizing social skill differences and promoting acceptance can reduce the pressure neurodivergent individuals feel to mask by supporting all children to be their authentic selves and be able to advocate for their own social and emotional needs.

AUTISTIC CULTURE AND SOCIAL SKILLS

As we mentioned in the previous chapter, culture can be described as "the beliefs, values, rituals and practices of any group of people." The idea of autistic culture has emerged in recent years as a way of recognizing the shared experiences of autistic individuals. Through a cultural lens, autistic individuals have begun to reclaim previously pathologized features such as stimming and the need for routine as simply autistic ways of being that foster a sense of belonging for many in the autistic community.

Just as other cultures have a set of social skills or conventions that are accepted or considered the norm within their community, it makes sense that autistic individuals would have their own set of social skills that are influenced by the way they see and interact with the world. While there isn't yet a universal definition of autistic social skills, there are several commonly agreed upon elements. It is important to remember, however, that these are generalizations that will vary between individuals.

Communication

The communication style of autistic individuals is often one of the first things that is highlighted when discussing autistic culture. Autistic communication tends to be direct, with quite a literal interpretation and use of language. Autistic individuals are naturally inclined to say exactly what they mean and be honest, will get right to the point when asked a question or sharing information, and will interpret questions or instructions literally.

Autistic individuals also place a lot of importance on facts and knowledge as opposed to opinions and can find it particularly challenging when other people have an opinion that's different to theirs, particularly if they believe that the facts support their own opinion on a particular topic.

Another feature of autistic communication is a reduced focus on nonverbal cues such as facial expressions and body language. Autistic individuals tend to place more weight on the words being said, rather than nonverbal communication, and often express themselves in ways that are different to their neurotypical peers. Eye contact is usually not a big part of communication either, and tone of voice and volume are often not noticed or regulated.

When in social situations, autistic individuals tend to have a real preference for deep and intense sharing of information, so a lot of autistic individuals are really not interested in making small talk and taking turns in conversation. They would rather jump straight into talking and connecting deeply about things that are important to them, and infodumping (sharing large amounts of information) about their passions.

It is also important to mention that some autistic individuals may also vary in their preferred mode of communication. For example, individuals who have the ability to use speech may at times prefer to use text, write, or use pictures to communicate and connect with other people. Others may use movie or TV scripts to express themselves.

Stimming

Stimming or self-stimulatory behavior is another autistic feature that is considered by many to be a part of autistic culture. Stimming encompasses a range of behaviors that include repetitive movements, object use or activities that usually involve a sensory element (e.g. hand flapping, rocking, spinning, humming, flicking a rubber band, listening to a song repeatedly, watching a movie repeatedly, etc.). Autistic individuals may stim for a variety of reasons including enjoyment or pleasure; arousal regulation (often through increasing or decreasing sensory input); and management of stress and anxiety. Neurotypical individuals may also engage in stimming, but it is more common and pronounced in the autistic community.

Intense interests

Intense or special interests, sometimes referred to as "SpINs," are commonly associated with the autistic experience. They are often a source of enjoyment and passion and also provide familiarity and comfort. For many autistic individuals, their chosen interest is all-encompassing, becoming the focus of play, conversation, thinking and learning. It is thought that this intense interest comes from autistic individuals having monotropic focus, a tendency for their brains to focus almost all their attention on one or two things, making it difficult to shift their attention to something else. Autistics often have times where they become fully immersed in their interest and lose track of time and what is happening around them. This is often called a flow state and is usually an enjoyable and often productive experience.

Empathy

Autistic individuals often show empathy by sharing an experience they have had that relates to what another person has been through. This is an autistic individual's way of communicating that they understand and feel for the other person. For example, a person might say that they have just lost a loved one, and in response the autistic individual might say that their cat died a few months ago. By doing this, they are sharing an experience to let the person know that they understand the feeling of grief and distress. Some autistic individuals also experience what can be referred to as "hyper-empathy," in which they are extremely sensitive to the emotions of others, often to a point to which they are unable to distinguish another person's feelings from their own. This can mean that when they are with someone who is experiencing big emotions, such as a child falling over and hurting their knee, they will also experience the same level of emotion and become equally as distressed as the child that is hurt.

Forming friendships

When it comes to engaging with friends, autistic individuals often love sharing experiences in parallel. This means that rather than feeling the need to engage in conversation or complete an activity or game together to connect, autistic individuals may prefer to do their own thing alongside a friend who is also engaged in their own activity. Being physically present with their friend, even when they are doing different things, creates a sense of connection and belonging. For example, two autistic children may sit together and read books, or play with playdough side by side, and just enjoy each other's presence without needing to talk.

Online friendships also seem to be more important to many autistic individuals. Connecting online with others can provide autistic individuals with an opportunity for direct and straightforward interactions that are not clouded by facial expressions and body language and can create a strong sense of belonging.

Reduced recognition of social hierarchy

Finally, many autistic individuals have an intense sense of fairness and justice and tend not to recognize social hierarchy. This means that they view everyone as the same and do not change the way they speak to or interact with others based on their age or position of authority. They also often feel compelled to speak up if they see someone treated unfairly, not just when it involves themselves.

WHAT DOES THIS MEAN FOR SOCIAL SKILLS TRAINING?

If we recognize and accept that autistic individuals have their own way of socializing rather than having "impaired" social skills; that there is a difference between autistic and neurotypical styles of social communication that leads to miscommunication and disconnect; and that teaching autistic children and adults to mask their natural ways of being to fit in with neurotypical social conventions can lead to poor mental health and wellbeing; where do we go from here? Is there still a place for social skills support?

The short answer to this question is "Yes."

With neurodiversity-affirming principles in mind, while we don't want to change the social skills of autistic children or their neurotypical peers, all children can benefit from learning about their own social styles and that there are ways of socializing that are different to their own. It is also important to learn how to be accepting of difference, and acceptance can be fostered by building understanding.

Social skills support, when directed at all children, can provide opportunities for the development of understanding and acceptance, and contribute to a safe and inclusive environment for everyone. The following chapters will explore how we can create neurodiversity-affirming social skills groups to support autistic children and their peers to thrive in their own unique ways.

CHAPTER 3

How Can Group Programs Support Autistic Children and Their Peers to Build Their Social Skills?

Social skills groups can provide a unique opportunity for children to develop skills and confidence in social interaction and build connections with peers in a safe and secure environment.

The use of group programs to support children and adolescents to develop skills and create a sense of belonging has been widely accepted as a therapeutic approach for many years and is considered evidence-based practice. Research regarding the most effective format and structure of group programs is difficult to find, however, likely due to the many programs available and the varied content and styles of delivery. In addition, children attending social skills groups often also attend other therapy services and receive support in other ways; associating clear outcomes with attending a social group in isolation is therefore challenging. And as social skills groups have traditionally taught neurotypical social skills to autistic children, research has often focused on the acquisition of these skills as an indication of effectiveness which is not consistent with neurodiversity-affirming outcomes.

What the current evidence does tell us is that children can benefit from small group activities with peers in a number of ways, including increasing their confidence in social settings, increasing their social awareness, improving social problem solving, and improving wellbeing due to a sense of connection and belonging. Further, successful groups can be run in schools or clinics or out in the community and can include all children.

FEATURES OF SUCCESSFUL GROUP PROGRAMS

Over the past 20 years, I have been lucky enough to run social skills groups both in schools and at our clinic, with children ranging in age from four to 12 years, and have seen first-hand the positive impact that social skills groups can have on autistic children and their peers. My approach has certainly changed throughout that time, with groups no longer being focused on children learning one way to socialize, and it is important to acknowledge that those early groups did not promote the message of acceptance that is now a priority in everything I do. However, the joy children have experienced sharing their passions with others and the friendships that have been formed have been a consistent and important reminder of the power of these groups in facilitating connection. Through my experience I have learned that some of the most important elements of a successful group program are ensuring that the children are engaged, that information is tailored to that particular group's needs, and that there is flexibility in how the information is presented.

Engagement

How to attract and hold a child's interest is probably one of the most important considerations for any educator, allied health professional or parent who is charged with helping a child build their skills and knowledge. No matter how important the message we are trying to communicate, if we don't grab a child's attention and keep them interested, they will not learn. This is especially evident when trying to teach children about something that they may not think is immediately relevant to them.

I have found that the best ways to keep children engaged in groups are to ensure things are going at a steady pace by not engaging in any one activity for too long, getting the children up and doing things rather than just sitting and talking, using games and sensory breaks to cater to their need for movement, and incorporating interests where possible to spark their interest and make information more relatable.

Another important element for engagement is to have fun. Using humor and finding your "silly" side can be a very effective way to help get children engaged and enjoying the group experience, especially for children in preschool and primary school.

Finally, it is extremely important to establish a relationship with each child in your group. If a child feels connected to you, and knows you like them and are interested in them, they are far more likely to engage in the program. Connecting with a child may be as simple as knowing what their interests are and asking about them each session or sharing some information about yourself that you think they might be interested in knowing. It is also important to be consistent in your behavior and reactions, and for a child to see that you mean what you say and therefore can be trusted. Brief, positive interactions and consistency can help a child trust and feel safe with you in the group environment, and if they feel safe and comfortable, they are likely to engage and learn more effectively.

Tailoring the material to group needs

While we do not always have comprehensive information about the children attending a group, having an idea of their basic skills and needs is very important in determining what information will be most beneficial for them to learn throughout a program.

When using a pre-written curriculum this can be difficult, as there are set topics and activities that need to be covered each session; however, if you are creating the program yourself, or can choose from a selection of pre-written plans, you can tailor the program to suit your group's needs.

You might gather information about a child's skills and needs by using a screening tool. Questions about likes and dislikes, communication preferences, situations that they find challenging, and what works best to support them can assist you to be prepared and create an environment that is going to be best suited to meet the group's needs and ensure they benefit from participating. Alternatively, you could introduce some basic principles or concepts in your first group session and gauge whether the group members are already competent in these skills or need to learn or review them before moving on to more complex ideas. For example, if you are running a group that is going to be focusing on understanding friendships, it may be important that children in the group already understand the different ways that people express emotions and communicate. If more complex friendship skills, such as social conflict resolution, are taught before a child has a basic understanding of social communication, they are unlikely to really benefit from the topic as they do not have the basic knowledge to build on. In this case, time may need to be spent establishing this foundational understanding before going on to the more complex subject matter.

Flexibility with the presentation of information

As with any setting in which children are involved, there are bound to be differences in language abilities, attention and learning within a group, and at times the suggested format for materials may not be suitable for your group members. It is important to be flexible and to "think outside the box" when it comes to presenting information to ensure the children in your group have the best possible chance to learn and develop their skills. For example, it may be necessary to use visual prompts or props to support understanding of concepts with some children, or to use video clips instead of books to introduce topics and keep the children in your group engaged. Or perhaps some music might be what works for your group best. Being flexible with the delivery of your material means that you can be sure that your group members are engaged, learning, and really benefiting from the group experience.

WHO CAN BENEFIT FROM SOCIAL SKILLS GROUPS?

While being social is something that comes easily to some children, for others it can be the cause of considerable anxiety and distress. This can sometimes be due to fear of doing the "wrong" thing, uncertainty about what is expected or what will happen, or a history of negative interactions with peers who have bullied or excluded them.

Research shows that autistic children and those with other disabilities are much more likely to be bullied or isolated than neurotypical children, and they have a higher incidence of mental health conditions such as anxiety as a result. However, having a lower incidence of mental health conditions and bullying doesn't mean that neurotypical children don't experience them at all. These are challenges that occur across the whole population at unsatisfactorily high levels and are an ongoing problem in preschools and schools everywhere. Social skills groups can offer children and adolescents who are anxious or isolated a safe and supportive environment in which to develop their skills and build up their experience of socializing in a positive way.

Now, it is important to note here that I am not talking about children doing social skills groups to learn how to behave differently so they "fit in" and are accepted or not bullied. I am talking about them doing groups to build their awareness of their own needs and the needs of others, and to have positive experiences with other children who will hopefully accept them for who they are.

But it is not only children with identified social challenges that can benefit from social skills groups. All children can benefit from learning about themselves and others, and developing awareness, tolerance and acceptance of difference. Group programs can be a great way to facilitate this.

BENEFITS OF GROUP PROGRAMS

The group environment lends itself to many valuable experiences that can support the social development of autistic children and their peers.

Gaining experience with peers in a naturalistic and safe environment

Attending a group program provides autistic children and their peers with the opportunity to gain experience in social interactions in a natural environment. While children may receive individual social skills support from therapists, practising these skills only with adults does not allow individuals to experience more typical social interaction with same-age peers. A group setting gives children the chance to interact more naturally with others, with the support of adults available when needed to assist them to safely manage any challenges that arise.

Building confidence in social interactions

In environments such as the classroom and playground, it can be hard for some children and adolescents to initiate and maintain social interactions with peers. This can further lead to problems developing friendships, as the opportunity to spend time getting to know classmates and connecting with them is limited.

When children participate in social skills groups, the small number of children along with adult facilitation provides an environment where connection with peers is supported and encouraged. This gives children the chance to find others who like the same things and enjoy completing activities together, which can often result in children arranging to meet up and spend time with each other outside of the group.

Meeting children who are similar to themselves

Many children and adolescents, whether they are autistic or not, have times where it can feel as though they are alone and that they don't belong. Coming to a group where they can meet peers who have experienced similar things or share similar interests can help give them a feeling that they are not on their own and provide them with a sense of belonging. Further, this feeling of belonging can contribute positively to a child's self-esteem and self-confidence, supporting a more positive overall view of themselves.

Meeting children who are different to themselves

It is common for children and adults to gravitate towards people we see as similar to ourselves. Similarity is often perceived as safe and predictable, qualities we seek not only to create connection but also to feel like we belong. For some individuals, meeting someone different may create curiosity and interest, motivating them to get to know the other person and better understand them. For others, perhaps those who are anxious about things that are new or unfamiliar, there may be times when someone who appears outwardly different to us in appearance or behaviors may create a feeling of uncertainty. This can then stop us getting to know others that are different, sometimes resulting in us making assumptions and having negative views of them. Being in a small group of peers with adult support provides children with an opportunity to socialize and get to know children they would not normally connect with. While this doesn't mean that everyone is suddenly going to be friends, it does create an atmosphere of familiarity and understanding that can assist children to be more tolerant and accepting of difference.

Improving social problem solving

Group programs also provide opportunities for children to problem solve social conflicts, with the support of adults, in a safe environment. Misunderstandings, disagreements and relationship breakdowns are unfortunately a mostly unavoidable part of being with and connecting with others, but they don't have to be unmanageable, and many situations can be resolved well when we have the skills. Adult facilitators can assist by "translating" what children may be thinking or feeling to aid mutual understanding, support emotional and arousal regulation, encourage consideration of other perspectives and build skills in identifying and resolving conflicts when they arise.

Involving parents and carers

Lastly, it is also important to remember that no child exists in isolation, and that the short time that a child spends in group may not result in skills continuing to develop and generalizing to other settings unless support and discussion of the skills occurs outside the group. Ensuring that parents, teachers and caregivers are provided with information about the skills being discussed in the group, and how they can help a child to further develop these skills, is very important in supporting the child to maintain and use the skills they have learned over time. This information can be provided in the form of handouts that describe the topic of each session and how parents can help, home tasks that are designed to be completed with the help of parents and that review the information presented in the previous session, and feedback about the child or adolescent's progress throughout the course of the group with suggestions for parents on how to support their child to further develop their skills at home and school.

CHAPTER 4

What Is Minecraft®?

Minecraft® is certainly not your average video game. Since its release in 2011, it has grown in popularity to become a worldwide phenomenon with over 200 million active monthly global users as of December 2024, and it shows no signs of slowing down. Minecraft is available on an increasing number of game platforms, including Windows, Mac, Linux, Android, iOS, Xbox One, Xbox Series S and X, Nintendo Switch, PlayStation 4 and 5 and more. There are two editions, Java and Bedrock, with Java being available only on PC, Mac and Linux, and Bedrock being available on most platforms. Bedrock enables players on a variety of devices to play in the same worlds, making it possible for friends and family members to play together across platforms.

So why is a simple video game so popular? Minecraft has been described as "digital LEGO®," as its open platform and "sandbox" quality gives players the ability to do and build just about anything. The term "sandbox" refers to the fact that players can virtually start with a blank canvas and create their own worlds and experiences, using building blocks, resources from the land and their own creativity. Players can choose to play in "survival" mode in which minerals must be mined, food grown and creatures defeated as part of an open adventure, or in "creative" mode in which they are free to make things with unlimited resources. It is a first-person player game, meaning that the player interacts directly with the game environment from their point of view, and can be played as an individual, or in a multiplayer option allowing for play with others on thousands of online servers.

The beauty of Minecraft seems to be its simplicity. In a 3D world of basic blocks and simple commands, virtually anything is possible. This simplicity also lends itself to creativity, flexibility and problem solving, which are important elements of learning. The learning and teaching potential of Minecraft has been recognized by its creator, Mojang, in the development of Minecraft: Education Edition®—a specific platform designed to enable educators to use Minecraft as a teaching tool in the classroom with administrative support and resources created and shared by users. Minecraft: Education Edition is currently used by millions of educators and students worldwide in subjects from art and history to science and maths, with new and innovative ways of using the platform being developed all the time.

HOW DO YOU PLAY MINECRAFT®?

The basic premise of Minecraft® really is straightforward. The world is made up of blocks or cubes that can be used to build all kinds of structures or can be mined for materials that are needed to make or "craft" useful items such as weapons or tools.

The game can be as complex or basic as the player wants. For example, a single player in creative mode has access to an endless supply of blocks and items and can make and do almost anything they want without being bothered by monsters or limited by materials. In contrast, a player in survival mode on a multiplayer server must mine for materials and hunt for food, while protecting themself from monsters and other players.

Further, in survival mode a player can be killed by monsters, other players or materials such as lava, and although they can respawn back into the game, they will lose any items and materials they have gathered, having to start from scratch again. Playing in survival mode therefore becomes a game of strategy and planning, in which storing or hiding materials just in case you respawn is necessary, and collecting weapons and protecting yourself is essential.

For more advanced users there are even more possibilities within the gameplay, including crafting complex items, taming animals, farming, trading with Villagers, using enchantments and potions to attribute special qualities to weapons or give players special powers (e.g. night vision), and building automated machines and devices using Redstone (the Minecraft equivalent of electricity).

CONTROLS

The different platforms used to play Minecraft all have different controls for movement; however, the way players move through the game is the same. Regardless of the platform, both the player's left and right hands are utilized, as one hand controls point of view, orientation and hand movements within the game (e.g. pick up, put down, break, hit, etc.), and the other hand controls direction and type of movement within the world (forward, back, left, right, jump, fly, etc.). Other controls for functions such as checking inventory and crafting materials are usually available through additional menus or buttons specific to each platform.

For example, when playing Minecraft on the Mac or PC, players utilize both the mouse and keyboard to navigate throughout the game. On the keyboard, the letter keys

W, A, S and D are used to move the player forward, left, back and right, respectively, while the mouse controls the direction your character is facing. The space bar is used to make the player jump or fly. The left shift key allows a player to descend from flight in a controlled way, or disembark from a boat or minecart, and the letter E key provides access to the player's inventory. As well as the mouse being used to control the character's point of view, the mouse left click controls hitting or breaking objects, and the right click controls the placement of objects and opening of doors and also allows a player to get into a minecart or boat, or mount an animal (e.g. horse, pig) to ride it.

ACCESSIBILITY

Minecraft® includes an Accessibility Menu with a range of options to accommodate the needs and preferences of players. For example, accessibility options in Bedrock edition include re-mapping controls to make them more intuitive to the player; text to speech narration for menus, screen text and chat; the ability to change font, size, color and background color for text to increase readability; and auto-jump to reduce repetitive button/key presses. The Accessibility Menu can be found by going to "Settings" in the main menu. There are also a number of game-wide changes that have been designed to improve the accessibility for all players including changing ore patterns (the texture of ore blocks) to make them more easily distinguishable for anyone who may have difficulty reading or perceiving colors.

The ability to play across different platforms also allows for individuals with different accessibility requirements to be able to play together in the same game using different devices. For example, a player who is more easily able to use keyboard controls can join a world with a peer who is more able to use a touchscreen and is playing on an iPad.

WORLDS

There are a number of different options available to Minecraft players regarding the worlds that they play in. Minecraft has infinite worlds, and you can randomly create a new one every time you play if that's what you choose. Alternatively, you can find a world and make it your own and even invite friends to join you in the game.

As I mentioned previously, the main world options are single or multiplayer. Single player provides you with a world that you are in completely on your own, while multiplayer places you in a world where other users are also playing and can connect with you. There are benefits and drawbacks to each kind of play. Single player mode allows you to play without having to be concerned about other players attacking you or trying to take your things, but is not ideal if you want to play and build with a friend. Multiplayer allows you to play with others and interact with them online, but in doing so allows people you don't know to chat to you and possibly "grief" you (i.e. deliberately annoy and frustrate you by repeatedly destroying your things and getting in your way).

An alternative option to using a public world is to create your own Minecraft® server and share the details with friends to allow access only to those who you know and want to play with. This can be done by downloading Minecraft server software and installing this on your computer or game console—which can be quite complicated if you are not tech savvy—or by signing up to Minecraft Realms. Realms allows you to have your own private server with up to three different worlds in it, and you choose who else can join by sending invitations to specific players. This avoids the problem of having unknown and unwanted people in your world, while still allowing you to play with friends. For the groups we run at my psychology practice, we use Realms to ensure that everyone can play safely and we are in control of the world and what is in it. This also allows us to change the world and its appearance to suit the activities that are going to be completed each session.

There are different versions of Realms for Bedrock and Java editions that have different limitations. Realms for Bedrock edition can be played across platforms and has options for either three players (Realms subscription) or 11 players (Realms Plus subscription) to play at the same time depending on licensing. In addition to more players being able to play together, the Realms Plus subscription also includes access to "Marketplace" where players can add skins, new worlds and other content. In Java edition, which can only be played on Windows, Mac and Linux, a Realms subscription includes access for 11 players at once.

BLOCKS

Minecraft wouldn't have its unique and iconic look without the blocks that make up almost everything in the game, from the landscape and buildings to the characters themselves.

The most basic of the blocks would probably be dirt blocks, which cover much of the surface of any Minecraft world and are easily broken. Other blocks vary in strength and availability, with some being commonly found in the landscape, such as stone, wood and sand, and others being rare and often only found if they are mined from underneath many layers of dirt or bedrock, such as diamond, gold and iron. Of course, when in creative mode, a player has simple and immediate access to all block types through their inventory, but in survival mode different blocks need to be mined and collected.

To create complex items such as weapons and tools, blocks need to be combined or crafted using a "crafting table," which is a special block that can be collected from a player's inventory or made using wooden planks. Once players have access to a crafting table, they can create a seemingly endless array of weapons, tools and objects from raw materials using recipes that combine the materials in specific ways. For example, to create an iron sword, the recipe requires two iron ingots (made from iron ore) and a wooden stick.

In addition to crafting, blocks also have another important role in gameplay—building. Players can create anything from simple houses or shelters out of wood, to complex and extravagant castles, and anything in between. Blocks are also often used by players to create "pixel art" or replicate real-life structures or pieces of artwork such as the Mona Lisa or the Eiffel Tower.

BIOMES

In the Minecraft® universe, each world can contain any number of biomes or environments, each with their own unique climate, flora and fauna, and geographical features. These biomes create regions within a Minecraft world such as deserts, forests, grassland, mountain ranges and jungles, which present players with a variety of different features to explore, and unique challenges to face. For example, on a mountain range, players may be faced with uneven, rugged terrain, and with rain and snow, making it difficult to build and mine. Alternatively, in a desert biome, the terrain may be flat but with limited plant life and water, making it difficult to find wood for construction.

Moving from one biome to another within a world provides players with opportunities to find minerals and materials that are unique to specific regions. Players can also encounter structures such as secret temples, complex cave systems and villages, which enable more varied and engaging gameplay.

MOBS

An explanation of Minecraft would not be complete without a discussion of the many creatures that exist in the Minecraft universe and can interact with players. These creatures are collectively referred to as "Mobs" and can be described as falling into three main types—Neutral, Passive and Hostile.

Passive Mobs cannot harm players, can sometimes be tamed, and will run away if they are attacked. Passive Mobs include farm animals such as pigs and sheep, tamed animals such as wolves and ocelots, and also Villagers.

Neutral Mobs will only attack if a player provokes them (e.g. if a player attacks the Mob first). Endermen, Spiders (in daylight) and Zombie Pigmen are all considered Neutral.

Finally, there are a number of Hostile Mobs that will attack players that are near them.

These Mobs are the ones that players in survival mode need to look out for and be prepared to fight, and include Creepers, Skeletons, Zombies, Wardens, Phantoms and Spiders (at night). There are also several Hostile Mobs that are further described as "Boss Mobs" due to them having more health than other Mobs which makes them harder to defeat and also having a larger range in which they can detect players and commence their attack. The "Boss Mobs" are the Wither, the Elder Guardian and the Ender Dragon.

As this chapter can really only be a brief summary of some of the things you might want to know about Minecraft®, I have included some useful websites at the end of the book that will provide you with tutorials and much broader knowledge if you would like to know more.

CHAPTER 5

Why Use Minecraft® to Build Social Skills?

The use of technology in education settings has increased significantly in recent years, with devices such as iPads and computers being widely used to assist with communication and learning in schools. Classrooms are invariably equipped with interactive white boards that are used for anything from taking the roll, to solving complex maths equations, to watching a documentary on space, and students are expected to be computer literate to enable them to research topics, create presentations and navigate educational programs designed to reinforce and extend the skills being taught within the school curriculum.

In this technological age, it makes sense that the use of devices such as computers and iPads would extend into the realm of therapy for autistic children and their peers. Computer programs and apps specifically created to teach skills such as regulating emotions and making friends are now widely available for use in schools, therapeutic settings and homes. Further, with the development and popularity of programs such as Minecraft®, teachers and therapists have discovered new and innovative ways to introduce concepts and engage students of all ages and abilities in learning.

So how can Minecraft be used to build social skills and what are the benefits of using a computer game as part of a social skills curriculum? As I mentioned in the Introduction, I have found that using Minecraft has proven to be very effective in supporting social skills development in children for a variety of reasons, not least of which is the lure of using technology and the novelty of playing a computer game while learning. A more detailed discussion of the many benefits of using Minecraft for teaching social skills will make up the remainder of this chapter.

TECHNOLOGY IS OFTEN MOTIVATING FOR CHILDREN

It seems that for many children, the lure of a screen is extremely motivating. Many autistic children and their peers are drawn to technology, and quickly become skilled in its use, resulting in them seeking to have time on a computer or iPad at any opportunity. As motivation is sometimes difficult to elicit, particularly in autistic children who tend to be monotropic in focus and have interest-based attention, using a format that is already motivating can assist with increasing engagement in activities and keeping children on task.

Understandably, for many children, talking about social skills is quite difficult, and learning about social skills is certainly not something they would usually choose to spend time doing. Therefore, using technology within a social skills group provides autistic children and peers with a motivating, enjoyable and less threatening way of building social skills and can support engagement and learning.

MINECRAFT® IS KNOWN AND PLAYED WORLDWIDE

One of the great benefits of Minecraft® is that it is a game that most children of school age have heard of and have played at one time or another. With its wide availability on platforms such as computers, game consoles and mobile devices, its global merchandizing including clothing, figurines and LEGO®, and the popularity of watching professional gamers play on YouTube, it seems rare to find a child who has escaped its influence completely.

Even for those who do not like Minecraft specifically, many children in their early years of schooling, from around five to 13 years of age, are very interested in computer games, and enjoy sharing their experiences of gameplay and their accomplishments with peers, sometimes even creating role-play games in the playground associated with their favorite gaming characters and adventures.

While some children may struggle to find interests they share with peers, which can sometimes impact on social connection and conversation, the popularity of Minecraft with school provides an interest that resonates with same-age peers. Minecraft can therefore act as common ground in the classroom and playground, giving children a common language in which to communicate and connect with their classmates.

MINECRAFT® IS A COMMON PASSION FOR AUTISTIC CHILDREN AND THEIR PEERS

As we've already discussed, autistic children often have passions for one or more subjects or activities that become the focus of almost everything they say and do.

These interests can vary from what may be considered unusual topics such as vacuum cleaners or air conditioners to interests more common amongst children such as horses, dinosaurs or trains. While interests can differ greatly between individuals, many autistic children count Minecraft® as one of those special interests and are extremely motivated to participate in anything Minecraft related.

Obviously, while non-autistic children may have a broader range of interests, and perhaps not experience the intense joy that an autistic passion brings for a topic or activity, many non-autistic children do love all things Minecraft.

This interest and motivation in Minecraft can be a powerful tool in the effort to build social skills and social awareness. It is widely accepted by most educators and allied health professionals that children demonstrate better engagement and more successful learning when they are interested in what they are doing. With interest comes increased participation, better attention and concentration, and enjoyment of the task, which should increase the likelihood that the information being presented will be retained and hopefully used later on.

Further, an interest in Minecraft does not just support engagement of tasks that are game-based but also encourages interest and involvement in learning about social skills concepts when they are presented with a Minecraft theme and involve Minecraft characters.

Using Minecraft therefore not only assists with motivation and engagement but also supports the successful learning of concepts and strategies presented within the context of the game.

SHARED INTERESTS ALLOW FOR MORE NATURAL INTERACTION BETWEEN GROUP PARTICIPANTS

For many autistic children, engaging in social interaction is hard work for a variety of reasons. However, within a group setting where the child knows that all the children in attendance like the same thing, it is much easier and less threatening for them to initiate interactions and have a conversation with a peer.

Not surprisingly, research suggests that when autistic children interact with others around a shared topic of interest, they are more relaxed and better able to communicate effectively. This may be due to them being better able to formulate comments, questions and responses based on their knowledge of the topic and having a more complex vocabulary around their interest, enabling them to express themselves more confidently. Further, for all children, sharing a common interest also provides the opportunity to connect with peers at a more meaningful level and gain enjoyment from social interaction, increasing the possibility of friendships being formed.

OPPORTUNITY FOR PARTICIPANTS TO SHARE THEIR KNOWLEDGE AND BE "EXPERTS"

In a game like Minecraft®, there is an endless supply of new commands, creations and skills that can be mastered while playing, and it is inevitable that, within a group of peers, there will be some children who are more skilled at Minecraft gameplay than others. Rather than this being a problem, this situation provides an opportunity for more skilled players to take on a helping and advisory role within the group, supporting other players when they are unsure how to do something.

Taking on the role of "expert" within the group can help a child increase their self-confidence and sense of mastery and develop a feeling of belonging. This can be particularly beneficial for autistic children, who may not get as many opportunities to demonstrate what they are good at or share their accomplishments with peers.

Being an "expert" also provides the opportunity for children to practice being patient, understanding and calm when helping someone, and to learn to adapt their communication so others can follow their instructions and successfully complete a task. The child receiving help also has a chance to practice their listening skills and can learn how to accept the help that is being given and any feedback regarding how well they are completing the task under instruction.

As it is likely that different children will have different skills and knowledge where Minecraft is concerned, any child within the group has the opportunity to take on the role of "expert" and share their knowledge at any given time.

OPPORTUNITY TO HAVE POSITIVE SOCIAL INTERACTIONS WITH PEERS

While playing Minecraft in the group, children don't just sit silently looking at their screen. Instead, they are engaged in dynamic social interactions with everyone around them including their partners, other group members and the staff. These interactions are usually based on the current gameplay the children are engaged in and might involve talking to another child about what they are building, asking for help, finding out what others are creating, or planning a joint project.

Facilitators can also encourage children to approach other group members for help or advice, perhaps ask a question about a peer's work, and support them to take turns on the computers or when using other materials and equipment. In this way, group members can practice using a variety of skills, including the specific skills we discuss in the session and other incidental social skills, as they are naturally required within the group setting.

LEARNING TO MANAGE CONFLICT

It is the nature of computer games being played by multiple children at once that at some point a conflict will arise due to the actions of one or more of the players. For example, a dispute may occur over the ownership of materials that have been found or the location in which a player wants to build, or there might be conflict following one player destroying the house of another in the game. These situations provide the perfect opportunity to support the players involved to problem solve and find a solution, and to regulate their emotions and behavior effectively.

In some cases, group members may be able to manage the conflict themselves, talking through the problem and how it might be fixed, especially when something has occurred by accident during play. At other times, an adult may be needed to support the children involved to express and regulate their emotions in a safe way, and if possible, consider the other person's point of view and potential solutions.

As you can see, there are many benefits to using Minecraft® to support social skills development in children. In the next chapter, I will take you through what you will need to set up your own Minecraft group at your school, practice or organization.

PART 2
Putting It All Together

CHAPTER 6

Getting Set Up

Given the popularity of Minecraft® and its worldwide use, there are many websites and tutorials available online that provide great information about setting up computers and Minecraft accounts, downloading Minecraft and getting started with gameplay. That said, there are a few things that we have learned along the way that will hopefully help you get set up and running your group stress free, and I would like to share these tips with you.

This chapter will briefly summarize some of the technical requirements you need to be aware of and refer you to more detailed information where required, as well as providing you with the tips and tricks that have helped us get set up for groups with minimal fuss.

PLATFORMS/DEVICES

Before you can start planning your Minecraft® group, you will need to decide what platform you are going to use. It is important to keep in mind that you will need to have at least one device for every two children attending the group, and all devices will need to use the same version of Minecraft. You may choose to have identical devices for consistency in setting up, such as just having computers, or to use a range of devices to allow for children who are not familiar with computer controls or who are more easily able to play using touchscreens.

For our groups, we have used a variety of platforms. For example, we have used five Mac desktop computers to accommodate ten group participants and also used a combination of Xbox consoles and iPads for a group of eight. Each set-up will have advantages and challenges, so it is important to think about the age and needs of the children participating and also what resources you will have available to you to run the group.

We have found that using computers can provide a great opportunity for interaction between group members due to the table set-up which allows for children to sit side by side and larger screens to support a shared experience. However, some children can find it difficult to sit up at a computer, and waiting for their turn may be particularly difficult for younger participants. In our group using Xbox and iPad, children were still able to join each other in the same world and play together, but they had more flexibility with whether they sat at the console or perhaps lay down on the floor with the iPad, and everyone having a device meant that pairs could work together in the Minecraft® world at the same time to complete activities and also during free time.

TECHNICAL REQUIREMENTS

To ensure your devices are able to support the most recent version of Minecraft, it is best to visit the Minecraft support page (help.minecraft.net) for the necessary specifications. There are also demo versions that can be downloaded to check whether your device is powerful enough to run the program.

You will need a stable and strong internet connection that is capable of carrying the load of several devices being connected to Minecraft at once, and you may choose to connect your computers by Wi-Fi or by a wired network connection. Where possible, it is best to have a dedicated internet connection for the program, as other users of the same network (e.g. staff members, other students) may experience slower internet access as a result of the group.

CREATING A MINECRAFT® ACCOUNT

To get started on your Minecraft journey, you will need to first create a Microsoft account and pay for and download Minecraft on each device. This is easily done from the official Minecraft website: Minecraft.net.

As there will be multiple players using Realms at any one time (one player on each computer or device), each device will need a different Microsoft account assigned to it. These can be created for free using a unique email address for each player.

When we first set up our computers for groups, we had to create five new email addresses to set up the player accounts. To do this, we set up individual email addresses on Gmail, but addresses can be created on any system you have access to (e.g. business email addresses, school accounts, etc.).

MINECRAFT® REALMS

Next, you will need to purchase Minecraft® Realms or Realms Plus on one computer using one of your Minecraft accounts. This account will act as the admin for the Realms server and will be used to control the various options associated with the Minecraft world that is used.

As mentioned earlier, Minecraft Realms is a version of Minecraft that allows friends to play together on a secure server where only invited players can join. We chose this platform for our groups as it allows us to control both which players are in the world and the characteristics of the world itself, without the possibility of external players getting access. Minecraft Realms is a subscription service in which users can sign up for just one month or for longer periods of time. One Minecraft Realms subscription using Java edition for PC or Mac allows for the user who purchased the subscription and ten other players to access the Realm. On Minecraft for mobile, console and Windows, a subscription for up to three (Realms) or up to 11 players (Realms Plus) is available using Bedrock edition. As we use Mac computers in some of our groups, we use the Java edition of Minecraft Realms, which is suitable for use on Macs and PCs but cannot be played together across other platforms. When using Mac, Xbox and iPad together we used the Bedrock edition. More detailed information about Realms and how to purchase a subscription is available at Minecraft.net.

CREATING/SELECTING WORLDS

Once your set-up of Realms is complete, you will usually have three worlds available to you that you can tailor to your needs.

Each world can be edited by selecting from several options which allow you to choose from a random world with qualities such as being "superflat" or containing structures, world templates that include places such as jungle villages or castles, and adventure templates which contain more complex settings. You can prepare each of the three worlds with the setting of your choice, but only one world can be used to play in at a time.

When we run groups, we often pre-prepare worlds to suit the activities that are planned for a session. For example, we may use a "superflat" world when group participants are going to be creating pictures or pixel art, or a mountainous world when the activity for the session is to build a rollercoaster.

It is important to note that if you require multiple worlds to be available to use in one session (e.g. one world to complete activities in and one world to have free play or destroy things), then you may need to purchase another Realm using another player's Microsoft account.

WORLD OPTIONS

Within each world, there are options available to change settings regarding the mode of play and the features that the world will include.

For our groups, we always play in creative mode so that no one's character can be injured or killed during play. We also always turn off "PvP," which stands for player versus player, so that players cannot attack each other. Other settings, such as Mobs or animals being spawned in the world, can be turned off or on as needed.

INVITING PLAYERS

The final step in the set-up process is to invite other players to join your Realm. This involves the player who purchased the Realm and is acting as "admin" selecting the option to invite players. The names of each of the other players that have been created for the group then need to be entered into the admin device (computer, Xbox, iPad, etc.) and an invitation will be sent to them. Once the other player logins are used to open Minecraft® on the other group devices and Realms is selected, an invitation will appear as a message at the top of the screen. Each invitation will need to be accepted to allow each player to access the world that has been created for the group. More detailed information about how to add players to Realms is available at Minecraft.net.

SETTING UP THE GROUP ROOM

When you are ready to run your group, it is important to consider not just the computers and devices, but also how you will set up your room. Ideally, you will have a large enough space to include computers or consoles on tables with two chairs at each table, and/or alternative seating for participants on iPads or tablets if needed; an area for group participants to sit on the floor during group discussions; and a space for movement breaks and alternative activities (see Chapter 7 for more information).

If using computers, they should be arranged to allow opportunity for interaction not just between each member of a pair, but between pairs as well. This provides more possibilities for positive social interaction between group members. For example, arrangement of tables in the shape of a "C" allows for interactions between all participants (Figure 6.1).

If you have limited space to run the group, or fewer than ten participants, you may need to arrange things differently. As long as the space is comfortable and workable for you, then it will be fine. Where possible, when the group room is small, it would be a good idea to prepare an alternative room or area to use as a "breakout" space for any children who need a break from the group for any reason.

FIGURE 6.1 SAMPLE ROOM SET-UP

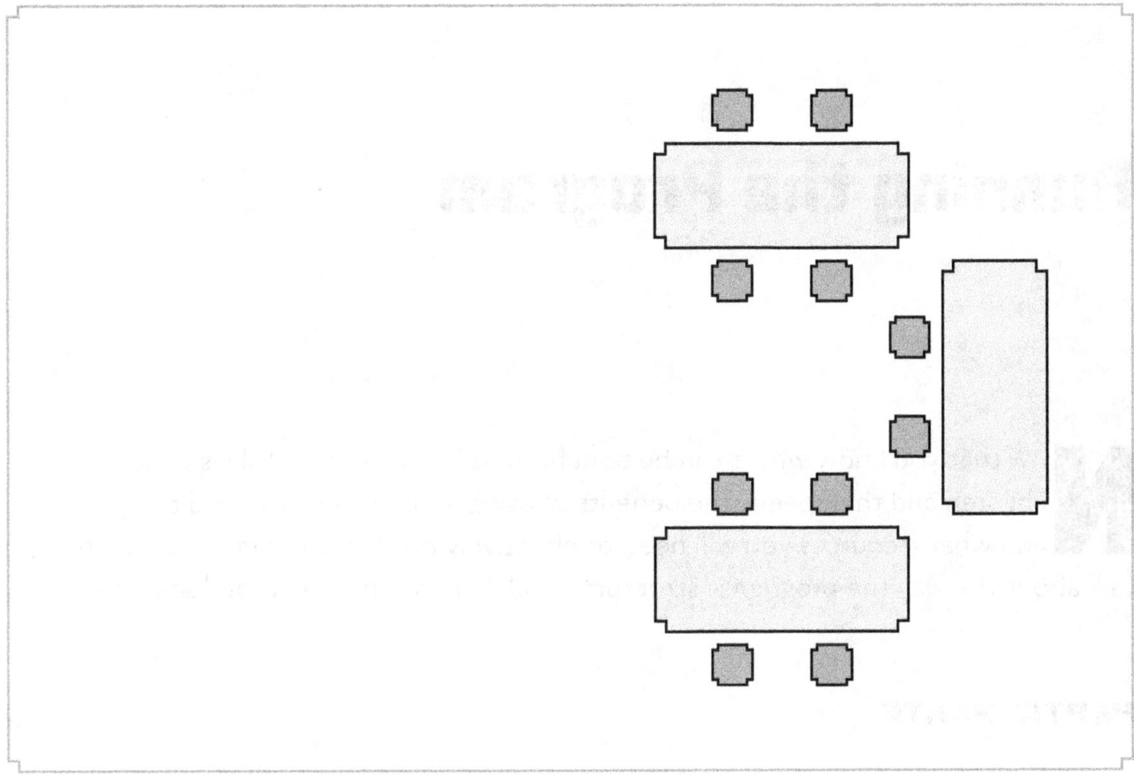

CHAPTER 7

Running the Program

Now that you know why it can be beneficial to build the social skills of autistic children and their peers, the benefits of using a Minecraft®-themed program, and what resources you will need to effectively run the program, it is time to talk about the way the program is structured and what a typical session looks like.

PARTICIPANTS

The program is designed primarily for children aged 5–12 years. It is suitable for any children who would benefit from building their confidence, awareness and skills in social interactions. As such, groups could include autistic children, children with other disabilities (e.g. Specific Learning Disorder, ADHD, etc.) and neurotypical children. Groups ideally consist of eight to ten children of similar age but could be smaller to accommodate children who require more support. At our practice, we usually arrange the groups according to year levels, with children in Prep/Foundation–Grade 3 (aged 5–9), or Grade 4–6 (aged 9–12), attending together; however, it would be appropriate for children all to be in the same year level or from a wider range of grades depending on the setting and the children wanting to attend.

STAFFING

For a group of eight to ten children, I recommend a minimum of two staff members, as this allows for one to facilitate the group while the other assists with providing support where needed. In a setting such as a school or with a smaller group size, one staff member may be sufficient; however, this would also depend on the needs of the children participating. We have been fortunate to have had access to psychology students from a local university who volunteer to assist with our groups, which has enabled us to have a higher adult-to-child ratio and provided participants with additional support during the group programs. Offering volunteer opportunities to university students in your local area who are completing qualifications in allied health or education can be a great way of having additional staff assist with running the groups.

PROGRAM STRUCTURE

The full program consists of 30 90-minute sessions. The sessions have been grouped into blocks of five that include the introduction of four social skills topics and a review session within each block. This structure ensures that the information presented in each session is reviewed at least once following its introduction and is viewed in the context of other social skills rather than being discussed in isolation.

While it is useful to run sessions in the blocks suggested, the program materials are also able to be used independently, allowing for facilitators to handpick topics that will specifically target the needs of their group members where required.

SESSION FORMAT

Each session follows a simple format that allows for the introduction of social skills topics and direct teaching by the facilitator, group discussion with participants, structured Minecraft® activities on the devices, and unstructured time that provides the opportunity for natural social interaction with peers. Depending on the children attending the group, it may also be necessary to schedule in movement breaks and alternative activities to cater to varied sensory needs and interests. Table 7.1 provides an example of the basic session structure and time allocated to each activity.

TABLE 7.1 EXAMPLE OF SESSION STRUCTURE

Time	Activity
5 min	Review Group Rules and Home Challenge from previous session
10 min	Introduce social skills topic and discuss with the group
10 min	Explain today's computer activity and discuss with the group
10 min	Player 1 starts activity on the computer
10 min	Player 2 starts activity on the computer
5 min	Movement break
5 min	Peer discussion of activities
5 min	Discuss social skills topic further (if appropriate) and explain plan for the next computer activity
10 min	Player 1 completes activity or has free play
10 min	Player 2 completes activity or has free play
10 min	Explain Home Challenge and give rewards
	Finish

If your group involves each child having access to a device rather than sharing, you may want to combine the time allocated to Player 1 and Player 2 in the above example or adapt the schedule to include other activities. The allocation of specific time frames to individual activities is helpful to keep the session flowing and ensure that essential information is covered; however, flexibility within the session is also important. For example, if participants are working well together completing an activity, it may be more beneficial to allow them to continue for a few minutes past the allocated time and have an extended positive interaction than interrupting them to follow the schedule exactly. Regardless of the specific topic of a session, any spontaneous positive social interaction between participants is something to be encouraged, as socializing naturally is the ultimate goal of any social skills group.

SESSION ACTIVITIES

Introducing and discussing the social skills topic

To introduce the topic for each session, I find it works best to let the participants know what we are going to be talking about and ask them what they already know about the topic (e.g. "Today we are going to talk about communication. Who can give me some examples of what communication is?"). This really helps the participants get involved from the beginning and helps direct further discussion of the topic. If your participants don't have anything to say, have a few suggestions of your own to assist them with ideas.

Using visuals to highlight the main points or concepts related to the topic is also useful, as you can break the skill down and discuss each point with an associated visual cue to enhance understanding and assist with keeping their attention. The main points for each topic are included in the handout for each session, and this can be used as the visual for the discussion. If you feel that using larger visuals will be most effective, you can print out the session handout on A3 paper to have more of an impact.

Once you have presented the main points that you want participants to understand, a discussion of why the skill is important, and when and where they might use the skill, helps to relate what they have learned to applications in real life. Ask for examples of when they have used the skills before and have your own examples and scenarios ready just in case. Having a white board and markers or paper handy to keep track of ideas can be really useful for this.

Explaining the Minecraft® activity and planning

The Minecraft® activities that are planned for each session are designed to provide an initial focus and structure for the participants when working on the computers or other devices with their partners. When introducing the activity for the day, talk to the participants about details such as what their creation might look like, what features might be essential to include, and what materials they might like to use. For some activities, participants will also need time to work with a partner to discuss and plan what they will do before they go to the devices to start their work.

Getting to work on Minecraft®

When it is time for participants to work on the devices, they should be encouraged to form pairs so they can complete activities together. You can do this by allowing participants to choose their own partners or by allocating children to specific pairs. If you have not met the participants before the first session, it is important to observe the dynamics between the participants and take note of any combinations of children that might be worthwhile encouraging or avoiding in future sessions to facilitate positive interactions.

If participants are sharing devices, they will need to establish who will have a turn first. This can be done through negotiation between participants or by using a method such as "Rock, Paper, Scissors" if an agreement can't be reached.

Once they commence work on Minecraft®, the focus is initially on completing the set task for the session. If sharing, the first participant is given a ten-minute block on the computers and then needs to swap with their partner so he or she can have a ten-minute turn. Following some further discussion in the middle of the session, each child will have the opportunity for another ten-minute block on their device.

Some children will need assistance and encouragement to focus and complete the activity or need support to understand what to do and how to do it. This is a great opportunity to encourage participants with more advanced Minecraft skills to assist their partners or other group members with the task and share their knowledge.

It can also be difficult for participants to wait for their turn while their partner is on the device. I usually encourage partners to stay together and support each other during the activities if possible; however, if a child needs to keep busy with another activity while their partner is on Minecraft, that is okay. Some ideas for appropriate alternative activities are included later in this chapter.

When the set task has been completed, participants are given an opportunity to engage in free play. This is best done by providing participants with an alternative world to log in to in which they can do whatever they want, without impacting on the creations of other group members. In my experience, free play time is often where you see participants increasingly engage in spontaneous social interactions with their peers. As they get to know each other through the sessions and build their confidence, participants often spontaneously create a challenge or activity to engage in (e.g. building a portal and fighting the Ender Dragon) and try to recruit others to assist them, providing the opportunity for them to work together and share enjoyment in achieving a goal.

Movement breaks

As mentioned earlier, movement breaks may be helpful and necessary for some children to assist them to regulate their arousal levels and to receive sensory input, stretch their legs and refocus. It is important to be aware of which activities are settling or calming for participants and which activities may heighten arousal. Typically, activities that involve firm pressure on joints (e.g. climbing, pushing, jumping and crashing) or rhythmic movement (e.g. rocking, swinging) are regulating and settling for most children, but there are always exceptions.

When I run my groups, we set up an obstacle course that includes crawling on a pile of cushions, rolling along a gym mat, bouncing on a mini trampoline and running and jumping into a crash mat. Alternatively, you could play a group game, do gross motor activities such as crab walks or pushing on a wall, or even do some yoga. Obviously, you will need to consider the amount of space you have and what equipment you have access to before deciding on movement break activities for your group. If you are not sure or need more ideas, consulting an occupational therapist can be useful.

Peer discussion of activities

Setting some time for participants to share what they have created in Minecraft® with each other provides them with an opportunity to practice and build their confidence socializing. Some participants may benefit from an adult helping to facilitate this interaction; they can assist by encouraging participants to share their thoughts, perhaps ask questions if they want to know more, and support understanding of others' perspectives.

Home Challenge

Providing an activity for participants to take home and complete creates an opportunity for them to think about and apply what they have learned outside the group environment. It also provides parents with an opportunity to assist their child with understanding around the topic. The Home Challenge for each topic is included in the handout participants take home after each session.

You will need to take a few minutes at the end of each session to show participants the handout and explain what is required to complete it. Then you can discuss the challenge at the beginning of the next session and ask participants to share their experience of completing the task or their responses to the questions that were given. Sometimes participants will be reluctant to speak in front of the group. In these situations, you can offer to share their response for them (if it is written down) or encourage them to listen to their peers while they share their ideas. Do not try to make them speak to the group if they don't want to.

Note that there will be participants who do not do their Home Challenge for various reasons. If this occurs, include the participant in the discussions as usual and assist them to reflect on how they might have responded if they had completed the task.

Alternative activities

Having additional activities available for participants is useful, particularly for children who have difficulty waiting for their turn or lose interest in working on the devices throughout the session. These activities provide an alternative opportunity for social interaction in a less structured way and also allow participants time and space for regulation on their own if needed. Activities could include Minecraft® coloring pages and word searches, Minecraft papercraft, board games, card games or craft (e.g. bead art, cutting and pasting, etc.). Many of the craft and coloring resources are freely available online to download and use. I have included some useful websites in Part 3 for your reference. You will also find a Minecraft-themed Snakes and Ladders game in Part 3 that can be printed for use during sessions.

SUPPORTING REGULATION AND MANAGING STRESS BEHAVIORS

Group Rules

Setting clear expectations and boundaries right at the beginning of any group is very important, so one of the first activities that needs to be completed in the first session is establishing Group Rules. Once agreed upon, these rules can be referred to and reviewed in subsequent sessions to help maintain a positive group environment.

When discussing Group Rules with participants, it is important to encourage ideas from everyone regarding what rules might be needed to ensure everyone feels happy and safe attending the sessions. As with other discussions, have your own ideas ready in case the participants are having difficulty thinking of suggestions, or if they leave something out that you think is important.

Some common rules that are worthwhile considering are:

- "Hands, feet and objects to yourself": This is a rule that most children have come across at school in some form to remind them to not touch or hit others.
- "If you make it, you can break it": This is a rule I always include in these groups, as it refers to damaging other people's creations in Minecraft. Basically, it is all right for a child to destroy something they have made themselves, but not all right to damage anyone else's structures.
- "One person talking at a time": It can be helpful to highlight that talking one

person at a time means everyone can have their voice heard and it is easier for others to hear what we have to say, rather than everyone talking over the top of each other.

- "Be kind": Although the concept of "nice" or "kind" can sometimes be difficult to grasp, most children are aware of the importance of not purposely causing someone distress. A discussion of what that might look like and asking participants for examples can be helpful here.

It is best to keep the number of rules to a minimum and to make them meaningful to the group to increase the likelihood of them being followed and seen as fair. Having a lot of arbitrary rules and trying to enforce them (e.g. insisting that all children enter the room quietly and making them come in again if they are too loud) will just create tension and a power struggle that will damage your relationship with the participants and potentially make the group experience challenging for everyone.

Visual supports

Many children, and particularly autistic children, experience anxiety when in new situations and with new people, so attending a group for the first time can be a bit stressful. Further, it can take a while for children to settle in and feel comfortable with a new group—perhaps several sessions—so it is important to provide a predictable and safe environment for them to operate in that reduces their feelings of discomfort.

The use of a visual schedule is a great way to reduce the anxiety of participants by making each session more predictable. A visual schedule most often involves a series of pictures representing each activity or part of a program, which are displayed vertically on a board or wall in order of their occurrence. This allows a child to look at the schedule and see what activities are going to occur, in what order, and when the session will be finished. For example, a visual schedule for a typical Minecraft® group might include: Welcome; Group discussion; Today's activity; Minecraft time; Movement break; Group discussion; Minecraft time; Home Challenge and Finish. Examples of visual schedule cards are included in Chapter 8.

Sensory supports

Autistic children often experience differences in the way they process sensory information, and this can impact on their ability to regulate their arousal level and emotions. Sensory differences can also be experienced by neurotypical children and those with other neurodivergent neurotypes or disabilities, so it is important to consider the sensory impacts of the group environment to support all participants that are attending. Sensory sensitivities or needs can make it very difficult for children to feel safe and regulated in the group, resulting in challenges with focusing during discussions and participating fully in activities due to discomfort or distress.

When considering making accommodations for sensory needs, a general rule is that it is easier to individually increase sensory input for those who need it rather than decrease, so starting with a group space that has a reduced sensory footprint is often best. You can do this by considering things like the lighting in the room, reducing harsh fluorescent or down lights with reduced wattage globes or light covers that diffuse the light. Not using cleaning products with strong fragrances and monitoring the temperature, as well as reducing clutter and wall decorations, can also make a positive difference.

Once the room environment has been considered, accommodations for individual sensory preferences or sensitivities can often be made more easily such as: offering multiple seating options including chairs, wobble cushions and beanbags; having headphones available to reduce background noise; encouraging the use of fidgets and weighted toys or other products to provide sensory input; and providing space to move and pace safely. Sensory accommodations can make a big difference to how well a group runs and the enjoyment and participation of all the children involved.

It is important to add that at times we will need to balance each child's needs and act to find the best possible solution which may not always satisfy everyone. For example, if a child needs to stim by squealing, and another child is upset by the noise, we need to find a way to support both children to have their needs met. This may be by supporting the child who is squealing to move away if they need to stim or encouraging the other child to wear headphones to reduce the noise. This is not about one child being right and the other wrong; it is acknowledging and accommodating everyone's needs as best we can.

Rethinking behavior management

Since I began my career working with children many years ago, my approach to what is often called "behavior management" has changed dramatically. In the previous edition of this book, and within my clinical work at that time, using reward systems to "encourage positive behavior" and implementing consequences was considered best practice. Discussion of how to encourage children to make "good choices," and what to do when an "inappropriate choice" was made, dominated conversations about behavior, with the responsibility to make changes and do better placed squarely on the shoulders of the children. I am pleased to say that I have left this approach behind and can no longer recommend it.

We now know that children develop the ability to problem solve and reason quite slowly, and that the prefrontal cortex, the part of the brain responsible for thinking, learning and executive functioning including impulse control, working memory, attention/concentration and emotional regulation, is not fully developed in most individuals until their mid-twenties. We also know that when a child (or adult) is extremely stressed or heightened, the prefrontal cortex effectively goes "offline."

This leaves the lower parts of the brain, that operate the survival system and are reactive to threat, in charge of responding to the situation effectively. And if the only responses available to the child at that time due to their "thinking brain" being offline are to run away or hit out, that is what they are likely to do.

When we use reward systems to promote more "appropriate behavior" we are often expecting children to take responsibility for behavior they can't physically manage yet, basically setting them up to fail. This is especially true for neurodivergent children who often have challenges with executive functioning throughout their lives. So instead of using rewards, it should be the responsibility of caring adults to set children up for success by acting preventatively to reduce stress and facilitate learning and growth. We can do this by forming strong relationships, avoiding power struggles and recognizing that, as Dr. Ross Greene says, "kids do well if they can."

One way we can better support children in our groups is to use what is known as the low arousal approach. This approach was pioneered by clinical psychologist Andrew McDonnell and is a more effective and affirming method for supporting children to reduce stress and frustration, and prevent escalation to aggression and distress. At its heart, the low arousal approach is about acting to de-escalate a situation before a problem occurs, focusing on effectively managing the moment in the best way possible without entering into a power struggle or trying to teach a lesson. This means that an adult may strategically "give in" to a child who is becoming distressed to prevent them escalating to meltdown. For example, if a child is becoming distressed because they are struggling to wait for a turn on a device and want a turn immediately, we might give them another device to use on their own (if there is one available) to de-escalate the situation rather than insisting that they have to wait. The rationale behind this is that, as we have already mentioned, when a child is extremely stressed their prefrontal cortex goes offline, which means giving in to what they want in order to stop the escalation is not going to reward the child for their behavior as some might suggest, but will instead keep everyone safe and allow the child the space they need to regulate.

Within this approach, adults are also asked to reflect on biases and attitudes that impact on how they respond to challenging situations. For example, we may think that the child needs to learn to wait and shouldn't just be given what they want. However, if we consider that the child may not yet have the ability to manage waiting and was doing their best with the skills they had, we might view the situation differently. If you are interested in learning more about this approach, please see the resources in Part 3.

CHAPTER 8

Session Plans and Handouts

This chapter includes detailed session plans for facilitators, and handouts to provide to participants and their families, as well as additional information to assist with preparing for and running each session.

All handouts and certificates marked with a ⟐ can be downloaded as PDFs from https://digitalhub.jkp.com/redeem using the code PHLJYPK

SESSION 1: COMMUNICATION

World set-up

The world for this session should be one in which the students can explore and find treasure. When using Minecraft® Realms, I usually choose a premade world such as "Raider's Refuge" which has a large pirate's hideout to use as a base, water surrounding it to sail in, and lots of different areas to explore.

You will need to spend some time before the session placing chests around the world and filling them with treasure. There will also be chests already located in different places throughout the buildings that you can utilize too. You can place items from your inventory including gold and iron ingots, diamonds, emeralds, swords, pickaxes and armor, as well as novelty items such as cakes or golden apples. Vary the amount of each item in the world so some are more common than others—this makes for some interesting conversation when students are discussing what they have found.

Minecraft® activity

The first activity involves students moving around the world searching for and collecting treasure from the chests that have been placed there.

The second activity is to craft a boat and then explore the water around the island. Students will need to use a crafting table and follow the recipe on the handout.

Main message

- There are many different ways to communicate.
- All communication is valid—there is not a "right" way to communicate.

Key points for discussion

- What is communication? Does everyone communicate in the same way?
- How do you communicate your thoughts and feelings to others? Words, actions, facial expression, body language, other ways?
- Do you ever find it difficult to communicate? When?
- What can we do if we are not sure what someone is communicating?
- What can we do if someone is having difficulty understanding us?

Skills to highlight during the session

- Sharing information
- Asking for clarification
- Giving instructions

Session Plan

Time	Activity
5 min	Welcome
10 min	Group Rules
10 min	What is communication? Talk as a group about how we communicate with others.
5 min	Discuss today's activity—exploring Pirate Island. Talk with the group about how to move around the island, what to look for, etc.
10 min	Player 1 explores Pirate Island and collects materials
10 min	Player 2 explores Pirate Island and collects materials
5 min	Movement break
10 min	Check inventory. Talk to others about what they have collected. Collect supplies to make a boat. Review crafting recipe.
10 min	Player 1 crafts a boat and explores the water
10 min	Player 2 crafts a boat and explores the water
5 min	Explain Home Challenge
	Finish

HANDOUT 1 Communication

What we did today

Today we practiced our Communication Skills during the following activities:

- With the group, we discussed the different ways we communicate and what communication can look like.
- With partners, we searched a pirate island for chests containing treasure.

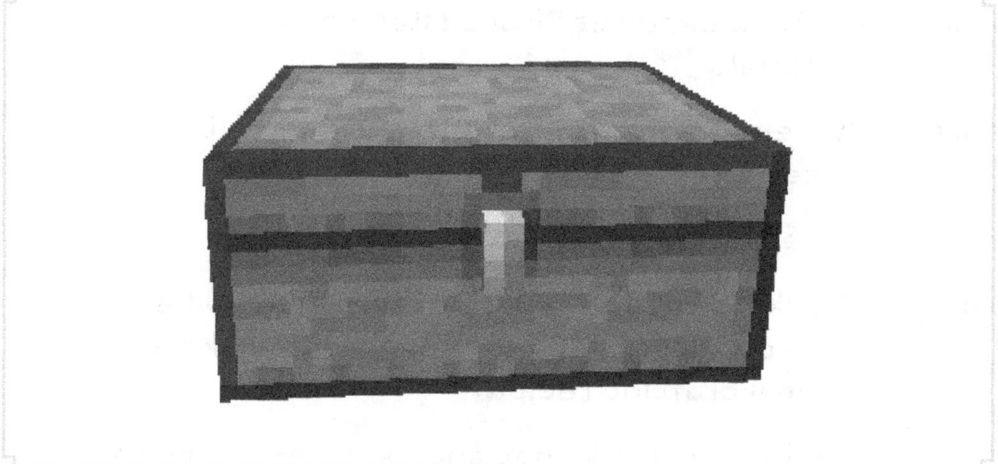

- With the group, we discussed what kinds of treasure were found on the island.
  - What did they find?
  - Where did they find it?
- With partners, we helped each other build boats and explored the water around the island.

How do you communicate?

Spoken words

Facial expressions

Gestures

Written words

Body language

Augmentative and Alternative Communication

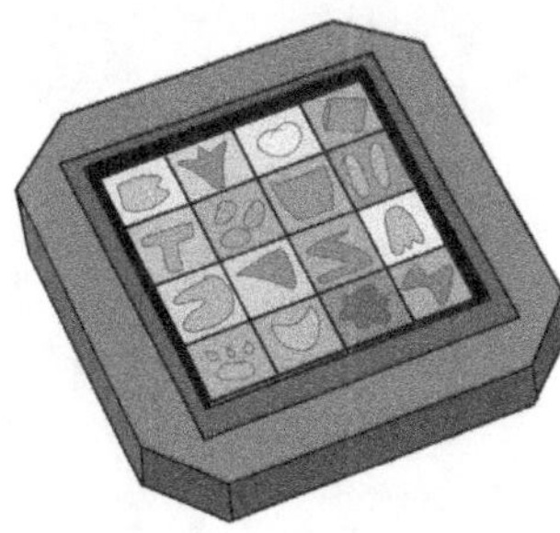

Pictures and symbols

HANDOUT 1 Communication

Why do we communicate?

- Share knowledge
- Learn
- Give feedback
- Show interest
- Ask and answer questions
- Express feelings
- Give instructions
- Make friends
- Indicate likes and dislikes
- Greet and farewell
- Get to know others

Home Challenge

Using your communication skills:

- Teach a family member (e.g. Mum, Dad, grandparent, brother or sister) how to craft a boat in Minecraft®.
- Then help them take the boat out on some water for a ride.

NB: You will need five wood planks to make a boat (and a wooden shovel if using Minecraft® on the iPad).

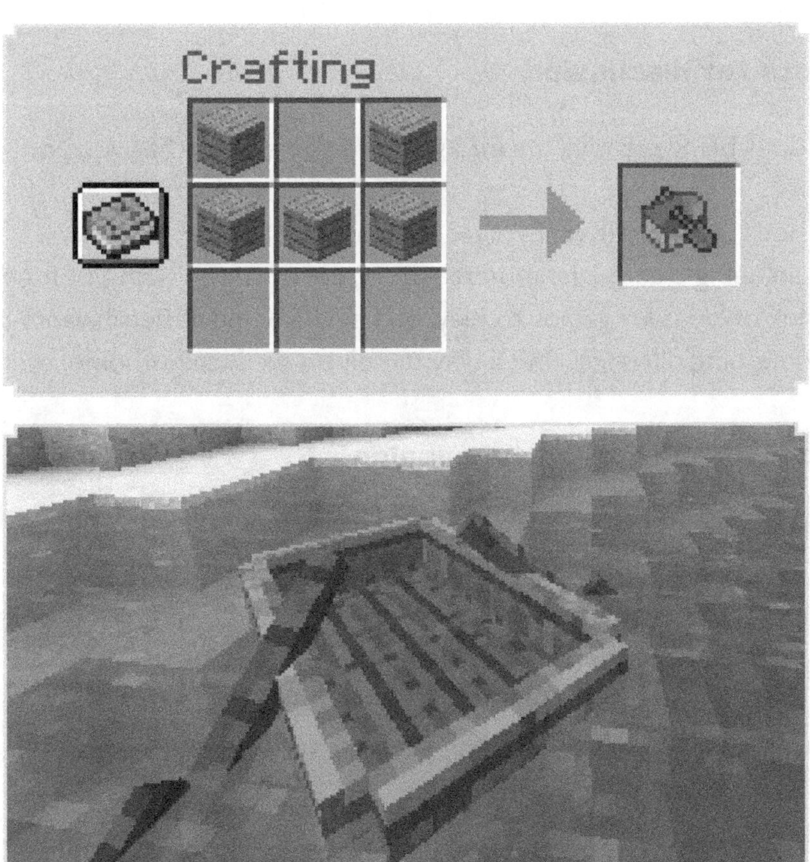

SESSION 2: CREATIVITY

World set-up

For this session, the world should be flat or at least have some flat areas so students can build. In Minecraft® Realms, you can generate a new world that is flat with no structures if required.

Minecraft® activity

The Minecraft activity for this session involves building a house and accompanying garden. Students can use all their allocated Minecraft time to complete a detailed design or can make something simpler and then engage in free play (preferably in an alternative world so they do not interfere with the work of others).

Main message

- There are lots of different ways to be creative (e.g. it is not just about art and craft).

Key points for discussion

- What does being creative mean? What are some ways that you are creative?
- What does being creative involve? —refer to handout
- How can being creative help us at school, at home and with our friends? E.g. think of ideas for games to play, be flexible when a friend wants to play something different, find a way to solve a problem at home, etc.

Skills to highlight during the session

- Flexible thinking
- Imaginative ideas
- Problem solving

Session Plan

Time	Activity
5 min	Welcome
5 min	Review Group Rules and Home Challenge
10 min	What is creativity? Talk as a group about what it means to be creative—flexibility, problem solving, imaginative.
10 min	Discuss today's activity—building a house. Talk with the group about what features a house needs, what it can be made of, etc.
10 min	Player 1 designs and builds a house
10 min	Player 2 designs and builds a house
5 min	Movement break
10 min	Discuss what features they have included in their houses so far. What else would be good to add?
10 min	Player 1 continues to build house and garden
10 min	Player 2 continues to build house and garden
5 min	Explain Home Challenge
	Finish

HANDOUT 2 Creativity

What we did today

Today we practiced being creative during the following activities:

- With the group, we discussed what being creative involves and how creativity helps us to think of ideas and find solutions to problems.

- Working with partners, we built houses in Minecraft®. We had to consider:
  - Where to build
  - Materials to use
  - Design
  - Features (number and type of rooms, furniture, etc.).

Creativity

How can we be creative?

Be flexible

Use your imagination

Think about different possibilities

HANDOUT 2 Creativity

Home Challenge

Using your creativity:

- Draw yourself as a Minecraft® character:
  - What would you wear? (e.g. clothes, armour, etc.)
  - What weapon would you have?

SESSION 3: FRIENDSHIP

World set-up

In this session, the world needs to be flat or feature large open spaces, to enable students to create pixel art.

Minecraft® activity

Students will create Pixel art for their Minecraft® activity, which involves using colored blocks to create a 2D image. Students may choose to create their own design or copy one. It is recommended that an assortment of designs be downloaded and printed before the session and be made available to the students for ideas. Pixel art patterns are available from many online sources including Google images using the search term "pixel art" and the name of an object or character (e.g. "pokemon pixel art").

Main message

- Friendship is a relationship or connection between two or more people who care about each other and like to spend time together.
- Friendship involves give and take from everyone involved—it is not just one way.
- Friendship can look different for different people.
- In a friendship, everyone should feel safe to be themselves.

Key points for discussion

- What is friendship? What qualities do you look for in a friend? —refer to handout
- How do you know someone is your friend?
- What do you like to do with your friends?

Skills to highlight during the session

- Shared interests in Minecraft
- Playing together
- Helping others
- Working together

Session Plan

Time	Activity
5 min	Welcome
5 min	Review Home Challenge
10 min	What is friendship? Talk as a group about what qualities they look for in a friend—similar interests, caring, listens, helpful, fun.
10 min	Discuss today's activity—creating pixel art. Talk with the group about how to create pixel art on Minecraft®—following a pattern, choosing correct colored blocks, etc. Each pair should choose two designs to make.
10 min	Player 1 creates pixel art
10 min	Player 2 creates pixel art
5 min	Movement break
10 min	Discuss what they have created. Was it easy/hard? How did they help each other with their art?
10 min	Player 1 pixel art and free play
10 min	Player 2 pixel art and free play
5 min	Explain Home Challenge
	Finish

HANDOUT 3 Friendship

What we did today

Today we explored ideas about friendship during the following activities:

- With the group, we discussed what we look for in a friend and how we can be a friend to others.
- Working with partners, we made pixel art in Minecraft®. We had to:
  - Decide on a picture to make together
  - Choose materials to use
  - Follow the pattern
  - Encourage our partners.

HANDOUT 3 Friendship

Friendship is a relationship between two or more people who care about each other and like to spend time together.

What qualities do you look for in a friend?

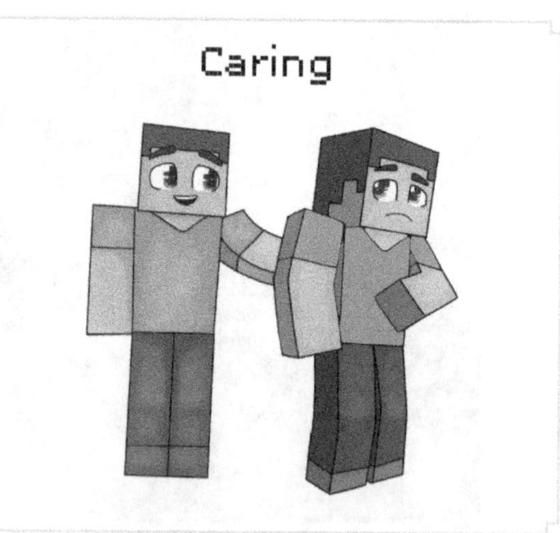

HANDOUT 3 Friendship

What do you like to do with your friends?

Talk	Exercise	Sit together
Play sport	Dance	Learn
Read	Relax	Play online
Listen to music	Make things	Watch

HANDOUT 3 Friendship

Home Challenge

Think about the qualities you look for in a friend. Are they different to those we've discussed?

What do you think are the three most important qualities in a friend? List them below.

1. ______________________________

2. ______________________________

3. ______________________________

What qualities do you have that make you a good friend?

____

____

____

____

SESSION 4: COOPERATION

World set-up

The world for this session is ideally one with some mountains or hilly landscape to support the construction of rollercoasters. Mountains give students an elevated starting point from which they can build their rollercoasters. Most randomly generated worlds should include some of these features.

Minecraft® activity

Building a rollercoaster is the main activity for this session. Before going on the devices, encourage pairs to start to talk about ideas and design their rollercoasters on paper. Once they have an idea of what they want to build, students can go onto Minecraft®.

While it is hoped that each pair will make one rollercoaster between them, it is alright for each student to make their own.

To construct a rollercoaster, students will need standard rails, powered rails and a minecart from their inventory. Standard rails can be used for any downward parts of the rollercoaster and corners, and powered rails should be used when uphill movement is required.

Main message

- Cooperation is working together to achieve a shared goal.
- Cooperating can help get things done faster and easier.

Key points for discussion

- What is cooperation? —working together to achieve something
- Why can it be good to cooperate? —makes things easier, faster, helpful, etc.
- How do we cooperate with others? —refer to handout
- When have you cooperated with others at home or school?
- What is compromising? —refer to handout

Skills to highlight during the session

- Listening to others
- Compromising
- Working together
- Regulating

Session Plan

Time	Activity
5 min	Welcome
5 min	Review Home Challenge
10 min	What is cooperation? Talk as a group about what it means to cooperate—work together to achieve something. Ask for examples of when the group have cooperated.
10 min	Discuss today's activity—making a rollercoaster. Talk with the group about cooperating to build with their partners. Discuss materials, placement, types of rails, etc.
5 min	Design rollercoasters in pairs
10 min	Player 1 builds rollercoaster
10 min	Player 2 builds rollercoaster
5 min	Movement break
5 min	Discuss what features they have included in their rollercoasters
10 min	Player 1 continues to build rollercoaster or free play
10 min	Player 2 continues to build rollercoaster or free play
5 min	Explain Home Challenge
	Finish

What we did today

Today we practiced the skills required to cooperate with others during the following activities:

- With the group, we discussed what being cooperative looks like and why cooperating can be beneficial.

- Working with partners, we made rollercoasters in Minecraft®. We had to:
    - Design a rollercoaster
    - Choose materials
    - Listen to each other's ideas
    - Compromise
    - Divide up tasks.

What is cooperation?

"Cooperation is working together to achieve a shared goal."

Share the work

Support each other

Listen to each other's ideas

Compromise

What is compromising?

I want... Compromise You want...

HANDOUT 4 Cooperation

Home Challenge

When do you cooperate?

- Find an opportunity to cooperate with your parents or siblings before our next session.
- Discuss the following questions with your family:
  - Did cooperating make the job easier or harder?
  - How did your parents or siblings feel when you cooperated?
  - How did you feel?

For example:

- Help your brother or sister pack up some toys.
- Prepare dinner with Mum or Dad.
- Build a LEGO® spaceship with your sibling.
- Help clear the dishes off the table after dinner.

SESSION 5: PUTTING IT ALL TOGETHER

SUMMARY SESSION

World set-up

The world for this session is ideally flat to allow room for the students to construct farmhouses and animal enclosures.

Minecraft® activity

In this session, students will work together to create a farm. Before going onto Minecraft®, discuss the types of features a farm may need and appropriate animals or crops to grow, and if possible, allocate a specific part of the farm to each pair.

Everything students may need for building a farm including fences and "eggs" to spawn farm animals can be found in the student's inventory.

Main message

- This session is an opportunity to review the content of previous sessions and apply what we have learned.

Key points for discussion

- What is communication?
- How can being creative help us at school and at home?
- What is a friend?
- How do we cooperate with others?
- What does compromising mean?

Skills to highlight during the session

- Communication (e.g. accepting different ways of communicating, asking for clarification, etc.)
- Creativity (e.g. flexible thinking, imagination, problem solving, etc.)
- Friendship (e.g. helping each other, being kind, sharing interests, etc.)
- Cooperation (e.g. working together, compromising, listening to ideas, etc.)

HANDOUT 5 Putting It All Together

Session Plan

Time	Activity
5 min	Welcome
5 min	Review Home Challenge
10 min	What have we learned about this week? ▪ Communication ▪ Creativity ▪ Friendship ▪ Cooperation Talk as a group about what we have learned and how we can use this information at school and at home.
10 min	Discuss today's activity—making a farm. Decide as a group what animals to put on the farm, who will build enclosures, who will spawn the animals, etc.
10 min	Player 1 builds farm
10 min	Player 2 builds farm
5 min	Movement break
10 min	Discuss what they have created. Was it easy/hard? How did they work together/communicate/create/support?
10 min	Player 1 builds farm or free play
10 min	Player 2 builds farm or free play
5 min	Give certificates
	Finish

HANDOUT 5 Putting It All Together

What we did today

Today we reviewed and practiced the skills we have learned over the last few sessions during the following activities:

- With the group, we discussed what we have learned and how we can use these skills at home and at school.

- Working as a team, we made a farm in Minecraft®. We had to:
  - COMMUNICATE clearly
  - Be CREATIVE and flexible
  - Support each of our FRIENDS
  - COOPERATE with each other.

SESSION 6: UNDERSTANDING POINT OF VIEW

World set-up

In this session, the world needs to be flat or feature large open spaces to enable students to create pixel art.

Minecraft® activity

Students will create Pixel art for their Minecraft® activity, which involves using colored blocks to create a 2D image. Students may choose to create their own design or copy one. It is recommended that an assortment of designs be downloaded and printed before the session and be made available to the students for ideas. Pixel art patterns are available from many online sources including Google images using the search term "pixel art" and the name of an object or character (e.g. "pokemon pixel art").

Main message

- Our experience of the world can be different to the experience of others.
- We may have different feelings about a situation than others do, and different ideas about what has occurred.
- We should try and be curious and accepting of other people's perspectives, even if they are different to our own.

Key points for discussion

- Why do Steve and Alex see the same Creeper in different ways? —refer to handout
- How can people sometimes see different pictures in optical illusions? —refer to handout (NB: Having additional optical illusions to look at can be useful.)
- What impact does having a different perspective have in social situations?
- Why is it important to respect another person's point of view?
- What is the difference between a fact and an opinion? —refer to handout
- Can we still be friends with someone who has a different opinion than we do?

Skills to highlight during the session

- Considering other opinions and points of view

HANDOUT 6 Understanding Point of View

Session Plan

Time	Activity
5 min	Welcome
10 min	Group Rules
10 min	Understanding point of view Talk as a group about how others might see and interpret things differently to us. Discuss why it is important to consider another's point of view.
5 min	Discuss today's activity—creating pixel art. Talk with the group about how to create pixel art on Minecraft® following a pattern, choosing correct colored blocks, etc.
10 min	Player 1 makes pixel art
10 min	Player 2 makes pixel art
5 min	Movement break
10 min	Fact vs opinion. Talk about the difference between fact and opinion and why it is all right for others to have a different opinion. Discuss examples of opinions and facts.
10 min	Player 1 makes armor and a weapon that they think is the best
10 min	Player 2 makes armor and a weapon that they think is the best
5 min	Explain Home Challenge
	Finish

HANDOUT 6 Understanding Point of View

What we did today

Today we learned about different points of view during the following activities:

- With the group, we discussed the difference between a fact and an opinion.
  - Is it okay to have a different opinion to someone else?
  - How can we accept another's opinion when we don't agree?
- With partners, we created pixel art. We discussed how pixel art looks up close and far away. Does it look different from another point of view?

- On Minecraft®, we each created our favorite armor and weapon for a character. We discussed how our choice might be different to our partner's.

HANDOUT 6 Understanding Point of View

How big is the Creeper from Steve's point of view?

What do you see in the picture below?

HANDOUT 6 Understanding Point of View

Opinion vs Fact

FACT

A thing that is known or can be proven to be true.

For example:

Creepers are creatures in Minecraft®.

OPINION

A belief, thought or feeling about something.

For example:

Minecraft® is fun!

HANDOUT 6 Understanding Point of View

Home Challenge

Fact vs opinion:

For each of the sentences below, underline the facts in green and the opinions in red.

- A skateboard has four wheels.
- Baby ducks are called ducklings.
- Basketball is a fun sport.
- The Earth is a planet.
- It's easy to win UNO®.
- Minecraft® is better than Terraria®.
- Swimming is a water sport.
- Cats make better pets than dogs.
- Jam tastes good on toast.

SESSION 7: HOW OUR BEHAVIOR CAN IMPACT OTHERS

World set-up

There are no specific requirements for the world for this session. Ideally, a world with several different areas or landscapes would be best (e.g. flat area, forest, mountains).

Minecraft® activity

In this session, students will create "machines" or cause-and-effect devices using Redstone. Some students may bring ideas from home or be very familiar with how to make certain items in Minecraft®, while others may need to see a recipe or example. It can be useful to have a few books with construction ideas and recipes for using Redstone on hand for the students who are not sure what to build.

Group activity

During the second group discussion time, students are encouraged to create a story as a group using Minecraft characters to illustrate how behavior can impact others. I find it easiest to have a white board or butcher's paper on hand and have the students contribute ideas for an event in the story and what will happen next, while I write the sequence of events down. The facilitator may need to prompt ideas to bring the story to a close if it is going for too long. Ideally, the facilitator will type up the story (with pictures if possible) and provide each of the students with a copy at the next session.

Main message

- What we say and do can have an impact on other people.
- That impact can often be considered positive or negative.
- Actions can have an impact, even when we don't have control of what we are doing. Sometimes the impact is planned and sometimes it is unexpected.

Key points for discussion

- What does it mean when we say that behavior has an impact?
- Can you think of situations where something positive or negative has happened due to something you did or said?
- What could the impact of Steve's behavior be on the Creeper?

Skills to highlight during the session

- Being considerate of others
- Being kind and helpful to others
- Considering the perspectives of others

HANDOUT 7 How Our Behavior Can Impact Others

Session Plan

Time	Activity
5 min	Welcome
5 min	Review Home Challenge
10 min	Talk as a group about how what we do and say can impact others—positive impact/negative impact. What does cause and effect mean?
10 min	Discuss today's activity—use Redstone recipes to create working machines.
10 min	Player 1 crafts with Redstone
10 min	Player 2 crafts with Redstone
5 min	Movement break
10 min	Make up a Minecraft® story together as a group. Consider the impact each action taken in the story has on the other characters.
10 min	Player 1 continues to craft with Redstone
10 min	Player 2 continues to craft with Redstone
5 min	Explain Home Challenge
	Finish

HANDOUT 7 How Our Behavior Can Impact Others

What we did today

Today we learned about how our behavior can affect others during the following activities:

- With the group, we discussed what consequences are and how what we do and say can affect other people.
- We considered that:
  - We can't control how another person reacts to what we do and say.
  - We can sometimes guess or predict how they might react based on our experience.

- Working with partners, we made devices using Redstone, which involves considering cause and effect.
- As a group, we developed a story based on Minecraft®, and discussed the actions of the characters and how they would affect each other.

HANDOUT 7 How Our Behavior Can Impact Others

How our behavior impacts others

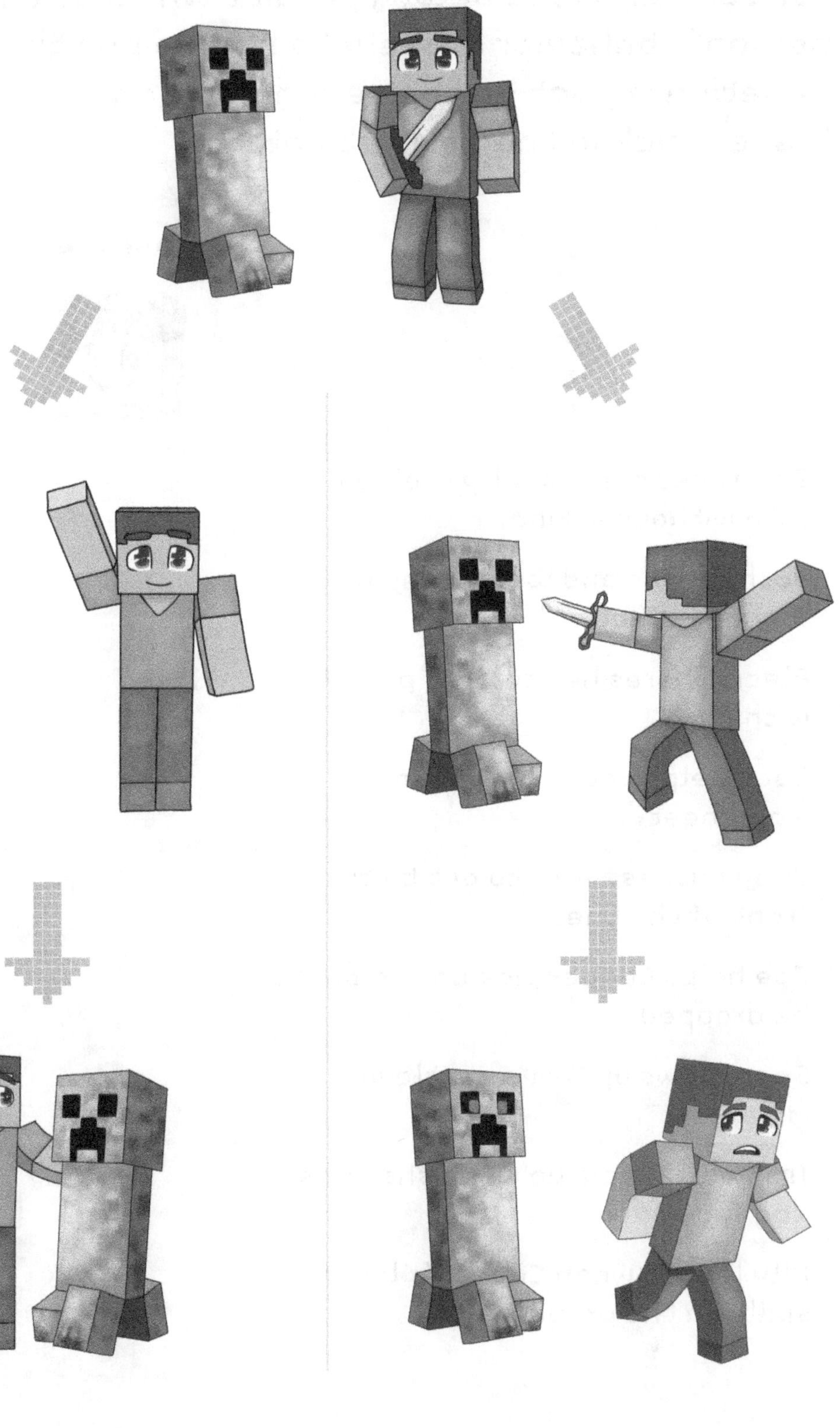

HANDOUT 7 How Our Behavior Can Impact Others

Home Challenge

For each example below, predict whether the first person's behavior is likely to have a positive or negative impact on the second person.
Place a tick in the correct column.

	Positive	Negative
Sam takes the ball Ally is playing with without asking.		✓
Josh frowns and looks away when Tom says "Hello."		
Alecia shares her colored pencils with Josh.		
Jack helps Sally with her math worksheet.		
Cody pushes Harry to get to the front of the line.		
Zoe helps Cooper pick up the books he dropped.		
Sean blows up Tom's castle in Minecraft®.		
Tim helps Alecia up when she trips and falls over.		
Ally laughs when Cooper's lunch spills on the ground.		

SESSION 8: BY ACCIDENT OR ON PURPOSE

World set-up

The world for this session is ideally one with some mountains or hilly landscape to support the construction of waterslides.

Minecraft® activity

Building a waterslide is the main activity for this session. Before going on the devices, encourage pairs to start to talk about ideas and design their waterslides on paper. Once they have an idea of what they want to build, students can go onto Minecraft®. While it is hoped that each pair will make one waterslide between them, it is alright for each student to make their own.

A waterslide can be made by cutting into the side of a mountain to create a crevasse in which water can travel down, or by constructing a slide with edges to hold the water. To add water, students can use a water bucket from their inventory and place it at the top of their slide to start the water flowing.

Main message

- Sometimes it can be hard to tell whether someone has done something by accident or on purpose.
- If it is an accident, someone made a mistake and didn't mean it. If it is on purpose, the person did it deliberately.

Key points for discussion

- What do we mean when we say someone did something by accident or on purpose?
- How can we tell that someone has done something by accident?
- How can we tell that someone has done something on purpose?
- How do you feel if you do something by accident that affects someone else? How might the other person feel? —refer to handout

Skills to highlight during the session

- Cooperation
- Being kind
- Recognizing if someone does something by accident
- Flexible thinking
- Encouraging others

HANDOUT 8 By Accident or On Purpose

Session Plan

Time	Activity
5 min	Welcome
5 min	Review Group Rules and Home Challenge
10 min	What do we mean when we say something was by accident or on purpose? What clues help us tell the difference? If we do something by accident, is it still our responsibility?
10 min	Discuss today's activity—building a waterslide. Talk with the group about how to build a waterslide. What features does it need? What can it be made of? etc.
10 min	Player 1 builds a waterslide
10 min	Player 2 continues building waterslide
5 min	Movement break
10 min	Show other groups the waterslides. What else would be good to add to make a waterpark/playground?
10 min	Player 1 builds playground
10 min	Player 2 builds playground
5 min	Explain Home Challenge
	Finish

HANDOUT 8 By Accident or On Purpose

What we did today

Today we learned how to recognize if something has been done by accident or on purpose during the following activities:

- As a group, we discussed what it means when someone does something by accident or on purpose and how we can tell the difference.
  - How might we feel if we do something by accident?
  - What can we do when something we have done by accident affects someone else?

- Working with partners, we designed and built waterslides. We had to:
  - Work together to design the waterslide
  - Encourage our partner
  - Recognize if someone did something by accident or on purpose.

HANDOUT 8 By Accident or On Purpose

When someone does something on purpose:

- They wanted to do it.
- They chose to do it.
- They thought about doing it before it happened.

When someone does something by accident:

- They did not mean to do it or want to do it.
- They did not choose to do it.
- They did not think about doing it before it happened.

HANDOUT 8 By Accident or On Purpose

By accident and on purpose

Sometimes when we do something on purpose, something happens by accident that we weren't expecting. For example:

- We might throw a ball inside on purpose that breaks a lamp by accident.
- We might jump on the couch on purpose and then fall off by accident.
- We might walk backwards on purpose and then bump into somebody by accident.
- We might use TNT to blow up a Creeper on purpose but then wreck someone's house by accident.
- We might sip a drink on purpose and spill it on our clothes by accident.

HANDOUT 8 By Accident or On Purpose

When we do something by accident that impacts us or someone else, we might feel:

sad	confused
playful	surprised
embarrassed	stressed
guilty	joyful
frustrated	bad

When we do something by accident that upsets us or someone else, we might:

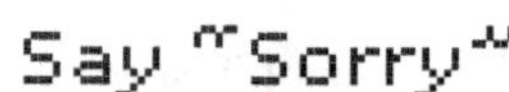

Offer to help

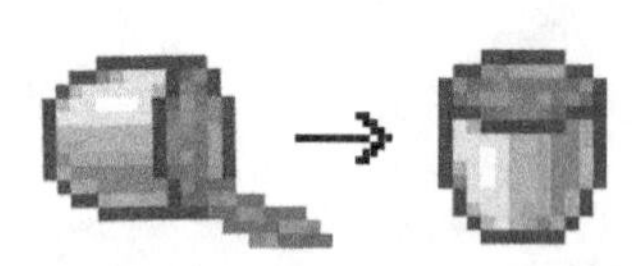

Ask for help

Try to fix things

Try to regulate

HANDOUT 8 By Accident or On Purpose

Home Challenge

Which of the examples below are accidents, and which are on purpose? Circle "**A**" for accident or "**P**" for on purpose.

- You are lining up to go into class. The person behind you bumps into you and you fall over. They say sorry and help you up.
  A / P
- You are playing basketball in the playground. Your ball rolls away from you and another boy picks it up. You ask him to throw it to you, and he throws it to the other side of the playground and laughs.
  A / P
- You are in art, and as you are reaching for a paintbrush you knock over a pot of glue. It goes all over someone's picture. You grab some paper towels and try and wipe it off the picture.
  A / P

SESSION 9: ASKING FOR AND ACCEPTING HELP

World set-up

There are no specific requirements for the world for this session, as students can craft or build items anywhere. Ideally, a world with several different areas or landscapes would be best (e.g. flat area, forest, mountains).

Minecraft® activity

In this session, each student will decide on an object to craft and teach their partner how to build it. Some students may bring ideas from home or be very familiar with how to make certain items in Minecraft®, while others may need to see a recipe or example in order to be able to instruct their partner in what to do. It can be useful to have a few books with construction ideas and recipes on hand for the students who are not sure what to build.

For each student's turn on Minecraft, their partner will be giving instructions on how to build a particular item. Even if the student already knows how to build something, it is important that they listen to their partner and follow directions rather than rushing ahead to finish on their own.

Main message

- There are different reasons why we might need help, and lots of different ways we can ask.
- If someone offers us help, we can decide to take their help or refuse.

Key points for discussion

- When might we need to ask others for help? (e.g. when learning something new, when hurt or confused, when something is difficult, etc.)
- How can we ask for help? —refer to handout
- When someone offers help, how can we accept or refuse their help? —refer to handout
- Do others have to accept our help when we offer it?

Skills to highlight during the session

- Listening to partners
- Following instructions
- Asking for and accepting help
- Offering to help others

HANDOUT 9 Asking for and Accepting Help

Session Plan

Time	Activity
5 min	Welcome
5 min	Review Home Challenge
10 min	Asking for and accepting help Talk as a group about when we should ask for help and how to ask. How should we accept help, or refuse help appropriately if we don't need/want it?
10 min	Discuss today's activity—crafting items. Talk with the group about helping each other to craft or build items. They can craft/build anything they like.
10 min	Player 1 teaches Player 2 how to craft items or build
10 min	Player 2 teaches Player 1 how to craft items or build
5 min	Movement break
10 min	Discuss what they have created. Was it easy/hard to take instruction from others? How did they help each other with their crafting/building?
10 min	Player 1 free play
10 min	Player 2 free play
5 min	Explain Home Challenge
	Finish

HANDOUT 9 Asking for and Accepting Help

What we did today

Today we explored how we can ask for and accept help during the following activities:

- With the group, we discussed when and how we might ask for help. We then talked about how to accept or refuse help when it is offered.

- Working on the computers, we took turns helping our partners to craft or build items of our choice. We had to:
  - Decide what to craft/build
  - Break down the task into steps
  - Listen and follow instructions
  - Try and be patient
  - Encourage our partners
  - Ask for help if needed.

HANDOUT 9 Asking for and Accepting Help

How to ask for help

Could you please help me?

Could you please tell me again?

Can you please show me what to do?

Note: Sometimes people will be more likely to help you if you use words like "please" which are considered polite in many cultures.

HANDOUT 9 Asking for and Accepting Help

How to accept or refuse help

Thanks. I'll give it a try.

Thanks. That's a good idea.

Thanks. But I can do it myself.

Thanks. But I'd like to try it my way.

Note: Some people like to say "thanks" or "thank you" to acknowledge the person offering help.

HANDOUT 9 Asking for and Accepting Help

Home Challenge

When we are trying something for the first time or learning something new, we often need some help.

- Write down four things you needed help to learn.

1. ____________________
2. ____________________
3. ____________________
4. ____________________

- Think of three people you can ask for help when you need it. Write their names in the spaces below.

1. ____________________
2. ____________________
3. ____________________

SESSION 10: PUTTING IT ALL TOGETHER

SUMMARY SESSION

World set-up

The world for this session is ideally flat to allow room for the students to construct houses for their village.

Minecraft® activity

Students will construct houses to create a village in Minecraft this session. As a group, students should discuss what types of houses or building are needed in a village, what materials they might use, who will build what type of building, and where they will build.

Main message

- This session is an opportunity to review the content of previous sessions and apply what we have learned.

Key points for discussion

- Why can it be helpful to consider another person's point of view?
- How can we recognize when someone does something by accident or on purpose?
- What are some ways to ask for help when we need it and accept or refuse help appropriately?
- How can our behavior impact on others at school and at home?

Skills to highlight during the session

- Accepting other opinions and points of view
- Being kind
- Asking for and offering help
- Considering the impact of our actions

HANDOUT 10 Putting It All Together

Session Plan

Time	Activity
5 min	Welcome
5 min	Review Home Challenge
10 min	What have we learned about this week? ▪ Understanding point of view ▪ How our behavior can impact others ▪ By accident or on purpose ▪ Asking for and accepting help Talk as a group about what we have learned and how we can use this information at school and at home.
10 min	Discuss today's activity—making a village. Decide as a group what buildings we need, who will build what and where, etc.
10 min	Player 1 builds in the village
10 min	Player 2 builds in the village
5 min	Movement break
10 min	Discuss what they have created. Was it easy/hard? How did they use the skills they have learned this week?
10 min	Player 1 builds village or free play
10 min	Player 2 builds village or free play
5 min	Give certificates
	Finish

HANDOUT 10 Putting It All Together

What we did today

Today we reviewed and practiced the skills we have learned over the last few sessions during the following activities:

- With the group, we discussed what we have learned and how we can use these skills at home and at school.

- Working as a team, we made a village in Minecraft®. We had to:
  - Consider others' POINTS OF VIEW
  - Think about the IMPACT of our ACTIONS
  - Understand when others do things BY ACCIDENT
  - ASK FOR and ACCEPT HELP when we need it.

SESSION 11: HAVING A CONVERSATION

World set-up

For this session, the world should be flat or at least have some flat areas so students can build their houses.

Minecraft® activity

The main activity for this session is to create gingerbread houses. These can be made from any materials. Students should be encouraged to use different colors and textures to create the look of a gingerbread house.

Main message

- There are lots of different ways to have a conversation.

Key points for discussion

- What are communication skills? —refer to handout
- What does having a conversation with someone involve?
- How do you like to communicate in a conversation?
- How do you find interests you share with someone else? —refer to handout
- Why can it be good to talk to your friends about shared interests?

Skills to highlight during the session

- Different ways of communicating
- Finding shared interests

HANDOUT 11 Having a Conversation

Session Plan

Time	Activity
5 min	Welcome
10 min	Group Rules
10 min	Having a conversation Discuss and review as a group how we communicate and what a conversation can involve.
5 min	Discuss today's activity—building a gingerbread house. Talk with the group about what features a gingerbread house needs, what it can be made of, etc.
10 min	Player 1 builds a gingerbread house with Player 2's help
10 min	Player 2 builds a gingerbread house with Player 1's help
5 min	Movement break
5 min	Discuss as a group what topics can be good to have conversations about. Introduce the idea of "shared interests" as some people prefer to talk about things they are interested in. Use real examples from the kids to find topics that would be "shared interests" for different people (e.g. friends, parents, siblings, etc.).
5 min	Find topics that are "shared interests" between Player 1 and Player 2
10 min	Player 1 continues to build or free play
10 min	Player 2 continues to build or free play
5 min	Explain Home Challenge
	Finish

HANDOUT 11 Having a Conversation

What we did today

Today we learned about what a conversation is during the following activities:

- With the group, we reviewed the different ways we can communicate and what a conversation can involve.
- We used our communication skills while helping our partners build a gingerbread house.

- With the group, we learned about how some people prefer to talk about things they are interested in and how we can find shared interests.
- Then we tried out finding topics in common with our partners and talking about them.

HANDOUT 11 Having a Conversation

Review: How do you communicate?

Spoken words

Facial expressions

Gestures

Written words

Body language

Augmentative and Alternative Communication

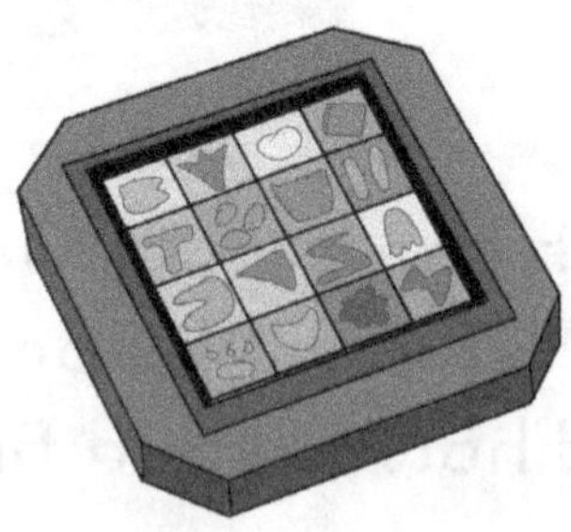

Pictures and symbols

A conversation is interactive communication between two or more people that usually involves talking and listening.

HANDOUT 11 Having a Conversation

Conversations can involve:

Sharing your interests and experiences

Infodumping

Making comments

Taking turns to talk

Talking about the same topic

Asking and answering questions

Talking about different topics

Listening to another person's ideas

HANDOUT 11 Having a Conversation

Some people prefer to have conversations about things they are interested in.

Steve likes:	**Shared interests**	**Alex likes:**
Mining	?	Horses
Trains		Diamonds
Creepers		Zombies
Building		Mining

Topics that Steve and Alex both like are **"shared interests"** and can be good to talk about.

Steve likes:	**They both like:**	**Alex likes:**
Mining	Mining	Horses
Trains	Mobs	Diamonds
Creepers		Zombies
Building		Mining

HANDOUT 11 Having a Conversation

Home Challenge

Shared interests:

Think about topics that you are interested in and also what interests a friend or member of your family.

Fill in the diagram below, putting interests that both you and your friend or family member share in the talking bubble in the center.

Try having a conversation about one of your shared interests.

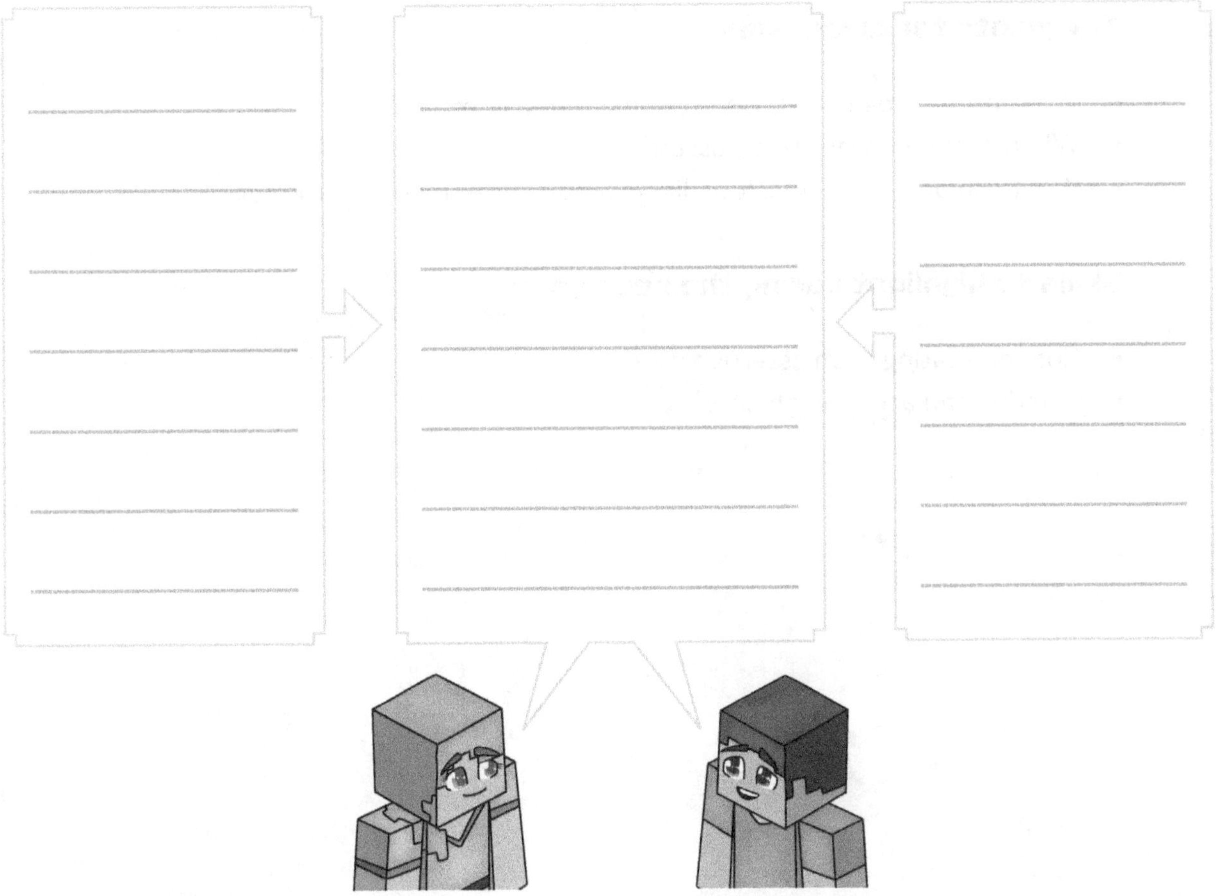

SESSION 12: BEING ASSERTIVE

World set-up

In this session, the world needs to be flat or feature large open spaces to enable students to create giant robots.

Minecraft® activity

For the activity this session, students will design and build giant robots. They should be encouraged to be creative and use their imaginations, and to use whatever materials interest them.

Before moving to devices, students should discuss as a group what kinds of features and materials could be used for building their robot. Then, in pairs, students can further discuss their individual designs before starting work on Minecraft®.

Main message

- When we are assertive in our communication, we are clear, confident and kind while stating how we feel or what we need so others will listen.

Key points for discussion

- What do we mean when we say someone is assertive?
- When might we want to be assertive?
- What can being assertive look like/sound like? —refer to handout

Skills to highlight during the session

- Communicating in an assertive way
- Offering and accepting help

HANDOUT 12 Being Assertive

Session Plan

Time	Activity
5 min	Welcome
5 min	Review Group Rules and Home Challenge
10 min	What do we mean when we say someone is assertive? How is being assertive more helpful than being aggressive or passive? How would you describe being assertive?
10 min	Discuss today's activity—making a giant robot. Talk with the group about what features a robot might need. What can it be made of? How high should it be? etc.
5 min	Plan robot with partner
10 min	Player 1 builds a robot
10 min	Player 2 continues to build a robot
5 min	Movement break
5 min	Show other groups the robots. What else would be good to add? How can you let others know you like their robot?
10 min	Player 1 continues to build robot or free play
10 min	Player 2 continues to build robot or free play
5 min	Explain Home Challenge
	Finish

HANDOUT 12 Being Assertive

What we did today

Today we learned how to be assertive in our interactions with others during the following activities:

- As a group, we discussed what it means when someone is assertive rather than aggressive or passive. We considered why it can be helpful to be assertive, and how assertive people look, talk and behave.

- Working with partners, we designed and built giant robots. We had to:
  - Work together to design the robot
  - Encourage our partner
  - Communicate in an assertive way
  - Find a compromise if we disagreed with our partner.

HANDOUT 12 Being Assertive

Assertive

- Calm
- In control
- Direct/Clear
- Honest
- Kind
- Confident
- Stands up for themself
- Considers others

Aggressive

- Tense
- Threatening
- Mean
- Insulting
- Puts others down
- Wants things their way
- Doesn't think of others
- Wins at any cost

Passive

- Withdrawn
- Nervous
- Puts others ahead of own needs
- Bossed around
- Doesn't speak up
- Avoids conflict
- Goes without

Home Challenge

Think about some characters you know from TV, movies and games that you would describe as assertive, aggressive or passive.

List at least one character that fits each of the descriptions below.

Assertive

1. ____________________ 3. ____________________

2. ____________________ 4. ____________________

Aggressive

1. ____________________ 3. ____________________

2. ____________________ 4. ____________________

Passive

1. ____________________ 3. ____________________

2. ____________________ 4. ____________________

SESSION 13: BEING PERSISTENT

World set-up

For this session, the world needs to have plenty of water in which to build submarines. An island or a location close to an ocean would be ideal.

Minecraft® activity

In this session, students will design and build their own submarines. These can be built completely submerged in water, or on the surface, and can be created using any materials. It could be helpful to provide pictures of a few different submarines for students who are unsure of what a submarine can look like.

Main message

- When we are learning something new, it can be frustrating when we can't do it straight away, but some skills require practice before we can master them. If we persist with the activity and keep trying, we can learn to do it with time.

Key points for discussion

- What is persistence? —refer to handout
- Why can it be good to keep trying if you don't get something right the first time?
- What is something you learned to do after persisting until you achieved it? (e.g. riding a bike, writing with a pen, learning a dance move, building an ender portal in Minecraft, etc.)

Skills to highlight during the session

- Persisting to complete a task
- Encouraging others
- Problem solving

HANDOUT 13 Being Persistent

Session Plan

Time	Activity
5 min	Welcome
5 min	Review Home Challenge
10 min	Talk as a group about what being persistent means and why it can be helpful when you are learning something new. How do you feel when you can't do something straight away? Why can it be good to keep trying if you don't do something right the first time? Or the second time? What can you learn/achieve after persisting for a while?
5 min	Discuss today's activity—building a submarine. Talk with the group about how to build a submarine, what features to include, etc.
5 min	Talk with your partner about what you would like your submarine to look like.
10 min	Player 1 builds a submarine
10 min	Player 2 builds a submarine
5 min	Movement break
10 min	Discuss what was easy/hard for them. What happened when you kept trying/persisted? What other objects would you like to be able to make in Minecraft®?
10 min	Player 1 free play
10 min	Player 2 free play
5 min	Explain Home Challenge
	Finish

HANDOUT 13 Being Persistent

What we did today

Today we practiced the skills required to be persistent when something is difficult, while completing the following activities:

- With the group, we discussed what it means to be persistent and how persisting when things get difficult helps us learn and develop new skills.

- Working on the computers, we took turns building a submarine. We had to:
  - Create a design
  - Break down the task into steps
  - Encourage our partners
  - Keep trying when things got difficult
  - Manage our frustration
  - Ask for help if needed.

HANDOUT 13 Being Persistent

Being persistent is when we keep trying to do or learn something, even when it is challenging.

Break the task down into steps

Ask for help

Keep trying

Take a break

Try a different way

Think "I just can't do it...

HANDOUT 13 Being Persistent

Home Challenge

Think about a time when you found something difficult but kept trying (persisted) until you could do it, then answer the following questions:

1. What were you trying to do?

2. How did you feel when you were finding it hard?

3. What happened when you kept trying?

4. How did you feel when you could do it?

SESSION 14: MANAGING CONFLICT

World set-up

For this session, the world should be flat or at least have some flat areas so students can build their playgrounds on an open area.

Minecraft® activity

The activity for this session is to create a playground. Each student will need to find an area to build on and to decide on what kinds of equipment they will feature (e.g. swings, slide, climbing fort).

Main message

- Conflict can occur when we disagree, argue or get back at someone who has upset us.
- We can experience conflict with parents, siblings, teachers and friends.
- There are things we can do to manage conflict in helpful ways.

Key points for discussion

- What is conflict?
- What kinds of situations can cause conflict with others?
- Who might you experience conflict with at home or school?
- What is the best way to manage conflict? —refer to handout

Skills to highlight during the session

- Listening to others
- Taking time to regulate if needed
- Compromising

HANDOUT 14 Managing Conflict

Session Plan

Time	Activity
5 min	Welcome
5 min	Review Home Challenge
10 min	What is conflict? Talk as a group about what conflict is. What are some examples of conflict they might have with peers, siblings and adults? What are some helpful/unhelpful ways to manage conflict?
10 min	Discuss today's activity—creating a playground. Talk with the group about what the playground could include. Discuss materials, equipment, etc.
5 min	Design playground
10 min	Player 1 builds playground
10 min	Player 2 builds playground
5 min	Movement break
5 min	Discuss what features they have included in their playgrounds
10 min	Player 1 continues to build playground or free play
10 min	Player 2 continues to build playground or free play
5 min	Explain Home Challenge
	Finish

What we did today

Today we discussed and practiced the skills required to manage conflict with others during the following activities:

- With the group, we discussed what conflict is, what causes conflict and what we can do when a conflict happens with family or friends.

- Working with partners, we built playgrounds in Minecraft®. We had to:
    - Design a playground
    - Choose materials and equipment
    - Find a good place to build
    - Manage any conflict that started about where to build, materials used, whose turn was next and others trying to help.

HANDOUT 14 Managing Conflict

What is the best way to manage conflict with others?

Take time to regulate

Share your perspective

Be assertive

Listen to others

Find a compromise

I want... You want...

Compromise

Ask for help

HANDOUT 14 Managing Conflict

Home Challenge

- Share two examples of conflicts you have had with others at school or at home.

- What did you do to manage the conflict? Was it helpful or unhelpful?

- Would you do anything differently next time?

SESSION 15: PUTTING IT ALL TOGETHER

SUMMARY SESSION

World set-up

There are no specific requirements for the world for this session, as students can build their castles in any location. Ideally, a world with several different areas or landscapes would be best (e.g. flat area, forest, mountains).

Minecraft® activity

For this session, students will design and build a castle. Students should discuss the features and materials required with their partners and find suitable locations for them to build separately or together before going onto Minecraft®.

Main message

This session is an opportunity to review the content of previous sessions and apply what we have learned.

Key points for discussion

- Do you like to have conversations with others?
- What does being assertive look/sound like?
- Why can it be good to be persistent and keep trying when something is difficult?
- How do we manage conflict with others effectively?

Skills to highlight during the session

- Communicating clearly and assertively
- Talking about shared interests
- Persistence with challenging tasks
- Asking for help

HANDOUT 15 Putting It All Together

Session Plan

Time	Activity
5 min	Welcome
5 min	Review Home Challenge
10 min	What have we learned about this week? ▪ Having a conversation ▪ Being assertive ▪ Being persistent ▪ Managing conflict Talk as a group about what we have learned and how we can use this information at school and at home.
10 min	Discuss today's activity—making a castle. Decide in pairs what materials are needed, who will build what and where, etc.
10 min	Player 1 builds a castle
10 min	Player 2 builds a castle
5 min	Movement break
10 min	Discuss what they have created. Was it easy/hard? How did they use the skills they have learned this week?
10 min	Player 1 builds castle or free play
10 min	Player 2 builds castle or free play
5 min	Give certificates
	Finish

HANDOUT 15 Putting It All Together

What we did today

Today we reviewed and practiced the skills we have learned over the last few sessions during the following activities:

- With the group, we discussed what we have learned and how we can use these skills at home and at school.

- Working with partners, we made a castle in Minecraft®. We had to:
  - COMMUNICATE our ideas in an ASSERTIVE way Keep trying and be PERSISTENT if the activity became difficult
  - MANAGE CONFLICT if we had a disagreement with our partner
  - Have a CONVERSATION with others about what we built.

SESSION 16: LISTENING TO OTHERS

World set-up

There are no specific requirements for the world for this session, as students can build their underground hideouts in any location. Ideally, a world with several different areas or landscapes would be best (e.g. flat area, forest, mountains).

Minecraft® activity

This session, students will build secret underground hideouts. Hideouts can be built by digging into the ground or side of a mountain or using an existing cave as a starting point. Encourage students to find ways of hiding the entrance to their hideout and consider what features a hideout would need inside.

Main message

- We all listen in different ways. It can be helpful to know the way we listen best.

Key points for discussion

- What are the different ways that people listen?
- Why is listening to others important?
- How do you feel when others listen to you?
- How do others feel when you listen to them?

Skills to highlight during the session

- Listening
- Communicating clearly

HANDOUT 16 Listening to Others

Session Plan

Time	Activity
5 min	Welcome
5 min	Group Rules
10 min	Listening to others Discuss as a group the different ways that we listen to others at home, at school and with our friends. How do you feel when others listen to you? Do you sometimes find it difficult to listen?
10 min	Discuss today's activity—building an underground hideout. Talk with the group about what features a hideout needs, what it can be made of, etc.
10 min	Player 1 builds an underground hideout
10 min	Player 2 builds an underground hideout
5 min	Movement break
10 min	Show each other the hideouts that have been built and have each child explain what they have done. Consider other features that would be good to add.
10 min	Player 1 continues building hideout
10 min	Player 2 continues building hideout
5 min	Explain Home Challenge
	Finish

HANDOUT 16 Listening to Others

What we did today

Today we learned about listening to others during the following activities:

- With the group, we learned about the different ways we listen and how listening can show others we are interested in them.
- We practiced listening while discussing ideas and building a secret underground hideout with our partners.

- Working with partners, we had to:
  - Work together to design our hideouts
  - Listen to our partners' ideas
  - Be curious about the different ways others listen.

Listening to Others

How do you listen best?

Looking at the person who is speaking

Looking at something else

Moving around

Staying still

Wearing headphones

Keeping fingers busy

Something else

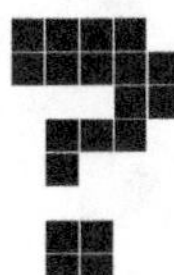

HANDOUT 16 Listening to Others

Home Challenge

Listening:

- Ask a family member or friend about how they listen best.
- Do they listen the same way you do or do something different?
- Write down some similarities and differences between your listening styles.

SESSION 17: RESPECTING DIFFERENCES

World set-up

For this session, the world should be flat or at least have some flat areas and preferably be in a cold biome so students can build their igloos in an open area.

Minecraft® activity

In this session, students will design and build an igloo. Students can use any materials in their inventory to build their igloo. Students should discuss the features and materials required with their partners and find suitable locations for them to build separately or together before going onto Minecraft®.

Main message

- Diversity and difference are just part of being human.
- It is important to treat others with kindness and respect and accept them for who they are.

Key points for discussion

- Diversity means "lots of different kinds of things."
- We are all human, but we look different and have different personalities.
- Why is it important to accept other people for who they are and accept their differences?

Skills to highlight during the session

- Accepting differences
- Being kind to others

HANDOUT 17 Respecting Differences

Session Plan

Time	Activity
5 min	Welcome
10 min	Review Group Rules and Home Challenge
10 min	Respecting differences Talk as a group about what diversity means: ▪ Diversity means "lots of different kinds of things." ▪ We are all human but we look different and have different personalities. ▪ Our differences make us unique and interesting. How are you the same as your friends? How are you different? How can being different be a good thing? When is it hard to respect the differences of others? How should we treat people who are different to us?
5 min	Discuss today's activity—building an igloo. Work with partners to discuss materials, features, etc.
10 min	Player 1 builds an igloo
10 min	Player 2 builds an igloo
5 min	Talk to others about what you have built
5 min	Was it difficult to respect the different ideas of your partner?
12 min	Player 1 continues to build or free play
12 min	Player 2 continues to build or free play
5 min	Explain Home Challenge
	Finish

HANDOUT 17 Respecting Differences

What we did today

Today we learned about respecting differences during the following activities:

- With the group, we discussed what "diversity" means and how we have more similarities than differences to others in the community. We talked about the importance of treating others with kindness, regardless of how they look, what they wear, how they speak or how they act. We also discussed how our differences make each of us unique.
- With our partners, we designed and built igloos in Minecraft®.

- We practiced respecting our peers' differences while building in Minecraft® and participating in other activities.

We are all human

- Our similarities make us part of our community.
- Our differences make us unique and interesting.
- Treat others the way you would like to be treated.
- Appreciate and respect the differences in others.

HANDOUT 17 Respecting Differences

Home Challenge

Think about a friend or family member that you are close to. What have you noticed that you have in common? What is different about each of you?

Use the boxes below to list how you and your friend/family member are similar and different.

What do I have in common with ______________________?

How are we the same?

How are we different?

What is good about being similar to others?

____

What is good about being different to others?

____

SESSION 18: FOLLOWING THE RULES

World set-up

There are no specific requirements for the world for this session, as students can build their towers in any location. Ideally, a world with several different areas or landscapes would be best (e.g. flat area, forest, mountains).

Minecraft® activity

Students will build towers to particular specifications for the Minecraft® activity for this session. The specifications are up to the facilitator to set but should include a few details that have to be featured in the tower. The main point of the task is that students follow any rules set by the facilitator. Specifications could include details such as the number of windows, building materials, the height or width of the tower, or decorations.

Main message

- Following rules helps us stay safe, play fairly and know what to expect in different situations.

Key points for discussion

- What places/situations have rules that you need to follow?
- What happens when you don't follow a rule at home or at school?
- Why do we have rules and why are they important to follow? —refer to handout
- How do you feel when others don't follow the rules?

Skills to highlight during the session

- Following the rules
- Listening to others

HANDOUT 18 Following the Rules

Session Plan

Time	Activity
5 min	Welcome
5 min	Review Home Challenge
10 min	Talk as a group about why we have rules and why it is important that we follow them. What places/situations have rules that you need to follow? What happens when you don't follow a rule at home/at school/in a game? Why are rules important? Why do we need them? How do you feel when other people don't follow the rules?
10 min	Discuss today's activity—building a tower. Talk with the group about building their tower to specific requirements.
10 min	Player 1 builds a tower
10 min	Player 2 builds a tower
5 min	Movement break
10 min	Discuss whether it was easy/hard for them to follow the rules. Are some rules easier to follow than others?
10 min	Player 1 free play
10 min	Player 2 free play
5 min	Explain Home Challenge
	Finish

HANDOUT 18 Following the Rules

What we did today

Today we learned about why we have rules and practiced following rules, while completing the following activities:

- With the group, we discussed why rules are important and what types of situations we need to have rules for.

- Working in Minecraft®, we took turns building a tower using specific rules about the size, materials and decoration.
- With the group, we discussed how it can sometimes be difficult to follow rules, and shared how we feel when others are not following rules at home and at school.

HANDOUT 18 Following the Rules

Why do we need rules?

To keep us safe

To keep others safe

To make things fair

To help us play

To help us make good choices

HANDOUT 18 Following the Rules

Home Challenge

Think about the kinds of rules you have to follow at school and at home.

On the lines below, write down two rules (one from school and one from home) and the reason you need to follow them.

Rule 1:

Reason for Rule 1:

Rule 2:

Reason for Rule 2:

SESSION 19: PROBLEM SOLVING

World set-up

There are no specific requirements for the world for this session, as students can build their sky houses in any location. Ideally, a world with several different areas or landscapes would be best (e.g. flat area, forest, mountains).

Minecraft® activity

In this session, students will build a floating village in the sky. Before going to the devices, the group should discuss the features that are important to include in their sky houses, and where they could be built. To make a house float in the sky, students will first need to build a tower of single blocks to the height they want, then build their house on top of it. Once their house is finished, they can destroy the blocks of the tower and the house will float.

Main message

- We all experience problems at different times. It can be helpful to use a five-step process to find solutions to problems when they occur.

Key points for discussion

- What is a problem?
- What kinds of problems do you experience at home and at school?
- How can we solve problems? What are some helpful/not helpful ways of solving problems?
- What are the five steps for problem solving? —refer to handout

Skills to highlight during the session

- Problem solving
- Communicating clearly
- Listening to others

HANDOUT 19 Problem Solving

Session Plan

Time	Activity
5 min	Welcome
5 min	Review Home Challenge
10 min	What is problem solving? Talk as a group about what problem solving is and when we might use it. What are some examples of problems that we need to solve? What are some helpful/unhelpful ways to solve problems?
5 min	Discuss today's activity—making a house in a floating village in the sky. Decide in pairs what materials are needed, who will build what and where, etc.
5 min	Design a sky house
10 min	Player 1 builds a sky house
10 min	Player 2 builds a sky house
5 min	Movement break
5 min	Discuss what features they have included in their sky house
5 min	Introduce Five Steps for Problem Solving
10 min	Player 1 continues to build a sky house or free play
10 min	Player 2 continues to build a sky house or free play
5 min	Explain Home Challenge
	Finish

HANDOUT 19 Problem Solving

What we did today

Today we discussed and practiced the skills required to solve problems during the following activities:

- With the group, we discussed what problem solving is, and the kinds of problems we might need to solve at school and at home.
- Working with partners, we built floating houses in the sky.

- With the group, we learned about the Five Steps for Problem Solving and how we can use these steps to solve problems in our everyday lives.

Problem Solving

Five Steps for Problem Solving

1. Identify the problem

2. Brainstorm solutions

3. Think—what would happen if...?

4. Decide on an action

5. Ask yourself—was it successful?

HANDOUT 19 Problem Solving

Home Challenge

Use the Five Steps for Problem Solving to solve a real problem you have experienced at home or at school.

1 **Identify the problem**

2 **Brainstorm solutions**

1.	2.	3.	4.

3 **Think—what would happen if...?**

1.	2.	3.	4.

4 **Decide on an action**

5 **Ask yourself—was it successful?**

SESSION 20: PUTTING IT ALL TOGETHER

SUMMARY SESSION

World set-up

For this session, the world should be flat or at least have some flat areas so students can build their bedrooms.

Minecraft® activity

In this activity, students will recreate their bedrooms in the Minecraft® world. Students can use any materials in their inventory to create a model of their bedroom, including important features, color schemes and furniture.

Main message

- This session is an opportunity to review the content of previous sessions and apply what we have learned.

Key points for discussion

- Why should we accept differences in others?
- How do we listen best?
- What places/situations do you have to follow rules?
- Why do we need rules?
- How can we use the Five Steps for Problem Solving?

Skills to highlight during the session

- Listening
- Being kind
- Following the group rules
- Problem solving when things go wrong

HANDOUT 20 Putting It All Together

Session Plan

Time	Activity
5 min	Welcome
5 min	Review Home Challenge
10 min	What have we learned about this week? ▪ Listening to others ▪ Respecting differences ▪ Following the rules ▪ Problem solving Talk as a group about what we have learned and how we can use this information at school and at home.
10 min	Discuss today's activity—recreating your bedroom in Minecraft®. Decide in pairs what materials are needed, who will build what and where, etc.
10 min	Player 1 builds their bedroom
10 min	Player 2 builds their bedroom
5 min	Movement break
5 min	Discuss what they have created. Was it easy/hard? How did they use the skills they have learned this week?
10 min	Player 1 builds bedroom or free play
10 min	Player 2 builds bedroom or free play
10 min	Give certificates
	Finish

HANDOUT 20 Putting It All Together

What we did today

Today we reviewed and practiced the skills we have learned over the last few sessions during the following activities:

- With the group, we discussed what we have learned and how we can use these skills at home and at school.

- Working with partners, we recreated our bedrooms in Minecraft®. We had to:
    - LISTEN to the ideas of our partners
    - RESPECT our partner's DIFFERENCES in the way they like to do and say things
    - FOLLOW THE GROUP RULES to keep everyone safe and happy
    - Use our PROBLEM-SOLVING skills to manage problems that occurred with our partners or while creating our bedrooms.

SESSION 21: TONE OF VOICE

World set-up

For this session, the world should be flat or at least have some flat areas so students can build spaceships in an open location.

Minecraft® activity

Students will design and build spaceships during this session. These can be built on the ground or in the air and can be created using any materials. It could be helpful to provide pictures of a few different spaceships for students who are unsure of what a spaceship can look like.

Main message

- Some people use their tone of voice to communicate their feelings when speaking to others.

Key points for discussion

- What do we mean when we talk about "tone of voice"? —refer to handout
- How do some people use their tone of voice to communicate how they are feeling?
- What can you do if a person's tone of voice and words don't match? —refer to handout

Skills to highlight during the session

- Noticing how others may use their tone of voice
- Communicating clearly
- Asking for and offering help

HANDOUT 21 Tone of Voice

Session Plan

Time	Activity
5 min	Welcome
5 min	Group Rules
10 min	Tone of voice Discuss as a group what we mean by "tone of voice" and how our tone of voice can sometimes change the meaning of the words we use (e.g. volume, pitch).
5 min	Discuss today's activity—creating a spaceship. Talk with the group about what features a spaceship needs, what it can be made of, etc.
5 min	Design your own spaceship. Talk to your partner about your ideas.
10 min	Player 1 builds their spaceship
10 min	Player 2 builds their spaceship
5 min	Movement break
5 min	Tone of voice What can we do if someone's words don't match their tone of voice?
5 min	Discuss ideas and improvements for spaceships with partners
10 min	Player 1 continues building spaceship and adds features (e.g. aliens, planets) or free play
10 min	Player 2 continues building spaceship and adds features (e.g. aliens, planets) or free play
5 min	Explain Home Challenge
	Finish

HANDOUT 21 Tone of Voice

What we did today

Today we learned about tone of voice and how some people use their tone of voice (e.g. volume and pitch) to communicate their feelings when speaking to others during the following activities:

- With the group, we discussed the different ways we can use our tone of voice to communicate with others and how our tone of voice can change the meaning of our words.
- We noticed the tone of voice of our partners while discussing ideas and building spaceships together.

- With the group, we learned about what we can do if we are not sure how someone is feeling when they are speaking to us.

Tone of Voice

What is tone of voice?

Your tone of voice is the way you use your voice when you communicate. We can think of tone of voice as being made up of volume and pitch.

Some people vary their tone of voice to communicate their feelings when they speak. Others don't change their tone of voice much at all, and communicate their feelings in other ways.

Volume

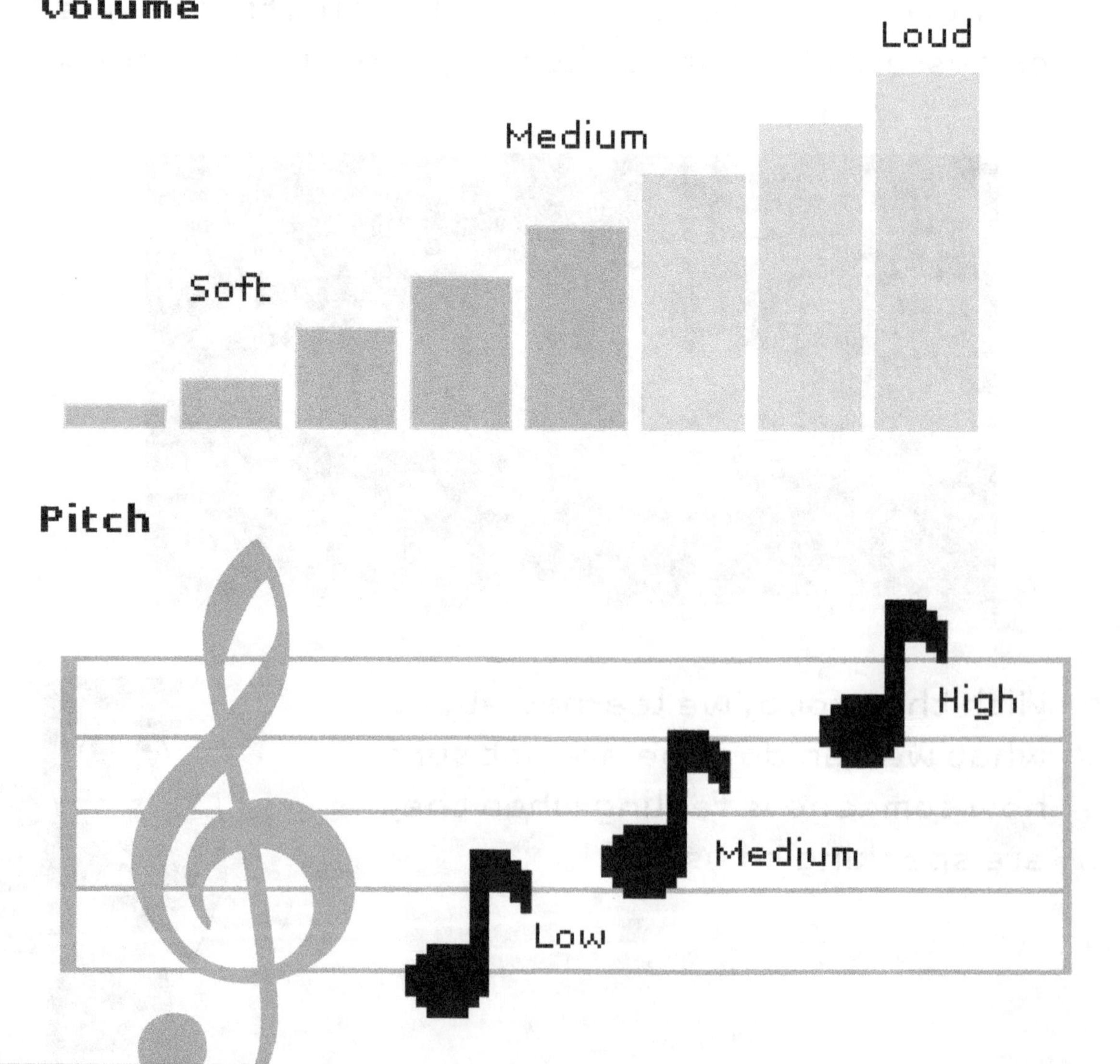

When feelings aren't clear

When you are not sure how someone is feeling when they are talking to you:

1. Look at the person's body language.
   - What clues are they giving with their facial expression and their body?
2. Look at the situation.
   - Where are you?
   - What is happening around you?
   - What was the person doing before they spoke to you?
3. Ask a question.
   - If you are still not sure how the person is feeling, ask them.
   - "I'm sorry but I can't read your tone of voice. Are you upset?"
   - "You sound a bit angry. Is there something wrong?"

HANDOUT 21 Tone of Voice

Home Challenge

With a family member, experiment with tone of voice by saying the following statements and questions with the emotions in brackets next to them.

1. I love ice cream. (bored, happy)
2. I have so much homework. (excited, worried)
3. I really like your hat. (annoyed, happy)
4. Why can't I go too? (sad, surprised)
5. I can do it myself. (angry, friendly)

Did your tone of voice change when you communicated different emotions or did it stay the same?

Did you notice changes in tone of voice when your family member communicated different emotions?

SESSION 22: SIZE OF THE PROBLEM

World set-up

For this session, a flat world will be required. You will need to spend some time before the session creating a maze. The maze can be built using any materials in the inventory and can be as simple or complex as you like.

If you require assistance with creating the maze, there are a number of free online maze generators that can be used to create a template to follow when creating the maze in Minecraft®.

Minecraft® activity

For the first activity in this session, students will find their way through the maze. Students should be encouraged to ask for help if they need it.

For the later activity, students will access a minigame that can be made available in an alternative world on Minecraft Realms or engage in free play. Minigames are available to choose instead of a world template in any Realm. There are a variety of games to choose from; however, once chosen for the world, only the selected minigame will be available for other players.

Main message

- Problems can come in many different sizes. Some problems may be easy to solve ourselves and some we might need help with.

Key points for discussion

- What kinds of problems might we face at home and school?
- How can we figure out what size a problem is? —refer to handout
- What problems might we be confident to solve ourselves and what problems might we need help with?

Skills to highlight during the session

- Problem solving
- Asking for and offering help
- Communicating clearly

HANDOUT 22 Size of the Problem

Session Plan

Time	Activity
5 min	Welcome
5 min	Review Group Rules and Home Challenge
10 min	Size of the problem Talk as a group about the types of problems we might face at school and at home. Discuss how we can figure out what size a problem is based on how easy it is to solve.
5 min	Discuss today's activity—finding their way through a maze. What size problem would it be if they can't get out? What can they do if they can't solve the problem on their own?
10 min	Player 1 goes through maze
10 min	Player 2 goes through maze
5 min	Movement break
10 min	Discuss what kinds of problems we might feel confident to solve ourselves and what problems we might need help with. Who can we ask for help?
5 min	Talk as a group about the next activity—playing a minigame
10 min	Player 1 plays a minigame
10 min	Player 2 plays a minigame
5 min	Explain Home Challenge
	Finish

HANDOUT 22 Size of the Problem

What we did today

Today we learned how to work out the size of a problem during the following activities:

- With the group, we discussed the types of problems we might face at school and at home, and how to figure out what size a problem is based on how easy it is to solve.
- We practiced figuring out the size of the problem while navigating a maze on Minecraft® and playing some minigames with our partners.

- With the group, we talked about what kinds of problems we might feel confident to solve ourselves, and which problems we might need help with.

HANDOUT 22 Size of the Problem

Thinking about the size of the problem

Problems come in lots of different sizes, and what feels big for one person might be small for another.

One way we can think about the size of a problem is based on how difficult they might be for us to solve.

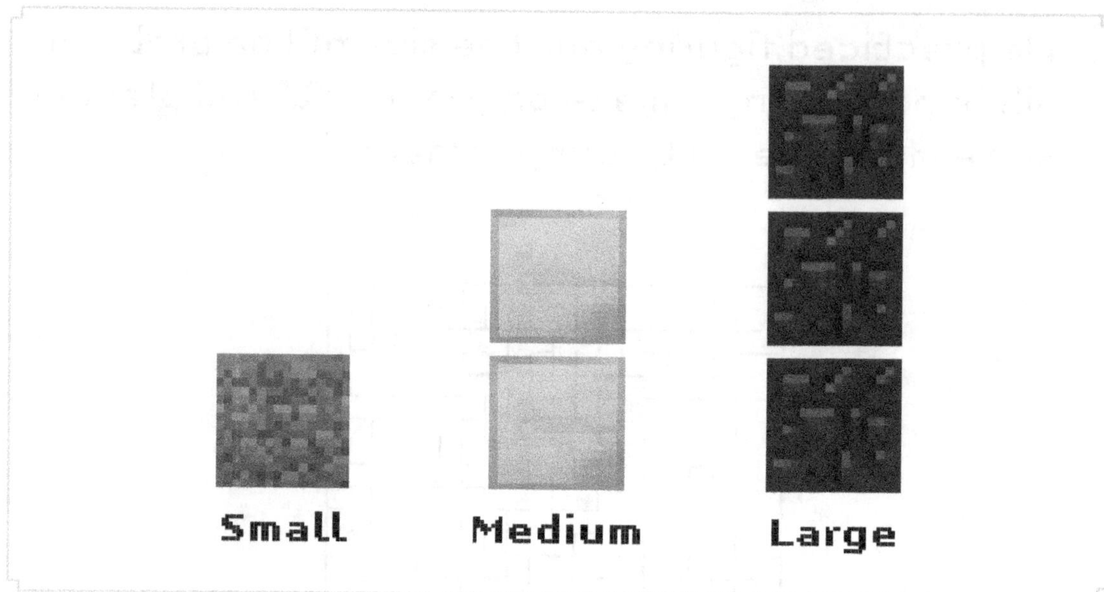

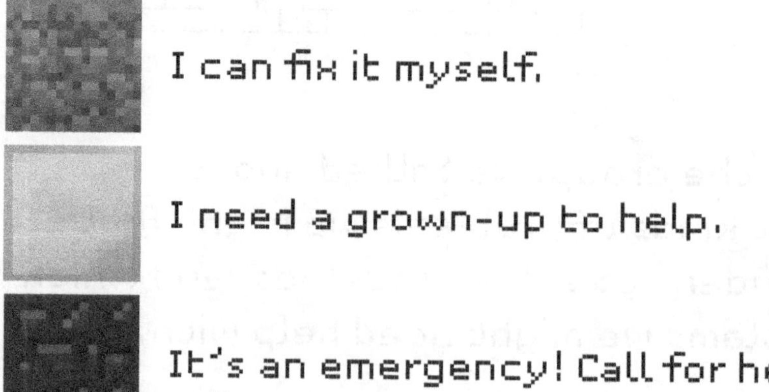

HANDOUT 22 Size of the Problem

Home Challenge

Sometimes when we have a problem, we can fix it ourselves. Other times we might need someone to help.

Think about a situation where you had a problem that you solved yourself.

What was the problem and how did you solve it?

____

____

Now think of a situation where you had a problem that you needed help to solve.

What was the problem and how did it make you feel?

____

____

Who did you ask for help? Were they able to solve the problem?

____

____

SESSION 23: BEING A GOOD SPORT

World set-up

In this session, the world needs to be flat or feature large open spaces, to enable students to create a pixel art trophy.

Minecraft® activity

Students will create a pixel art trophy for their Minecraft® activity. Students may choose to create their own design or copy one. It is recommended that an assortment of designs be downloaded and printed before the session and be made available to the students for ideas.

Main message

- Being a good sport means treating others with kindness and respect whether we win or lose.
- We might feel upset or disappointed if we lose. It is good to take a break if we are feeling upset.

Key points for discussion

- What does it mean to be a "good sport"? —refer to handout
- Why should we try to be a good sport when playing with others?
- How do we feel when we win or lose?
- What can we do if someone is being a bad sport? —refer to handout

Skills to highlight during the session

- Being a good sport while playing
- Communicating clearly
- Being kind

HANDOUT 23 Being a Good Sport

Session Plan

Time	Activity
5 min	Welcome
5 min	Review Home Challenge
10 min	Talk as a group about what it means to be a good sport. When is it important to be a good sport (winning and losing)? What does being a good sport look like? How does it feel when we win or lose?
5 min	Discuss today's activity—making a pixel art trophy
10 min	Player 1 builds a trophy (pixel art)
10 min	Player 2 builds a trophy (pixel art)
5 min	Movement break
5 min	Play Minecraft® Snakes and Ladders with a partner
10 min	Discuss how we should react when someone we are playing with is not being a good sport. Has anyone had that experience before? What should we do or say? Is it hard to stay calm?
10 min	Player 1 free play or board games
10 min	Player 2 free play or board games
5 min	Explain Home Challenge
	Finish

HANDOUT 23 Being a Good Sport

What we did today

Today we learned about what being a good sport involves and why it is important, while completing the following activities:

- With the group, we discussed what a good sport does when they win or lose a game.
- Working on devices, we created a winner's trophy with pixel art. We also played some board games with our friends. We practiced being good sports while playing together.

- With the group, we discussed how we can respond when someone we are playing with is cheating, changing the rules or being mean.

HANDOUT 23 Being a Good Sport

Play fair

Follow the rules

1. Hands, feet and objects to yourself.
2. If you make it, you can break it.

Encourage others

Accept the referee's decision

Be kind to the losers

Congratulate the winners

Take a break if you feel upset

HANDOUT 23 Being a Good Sport

What to do if someone you are playing with is not being a good sport.

1. Try to stay calm.

2. Try to talk about the problem.

3. Walk away.

4. Ask an adult for help.

HANDOUT 23 Being a Good Sport

Home Challenge

Play the "Minecraft® Snakes and Ladders" game with a family member or friend.

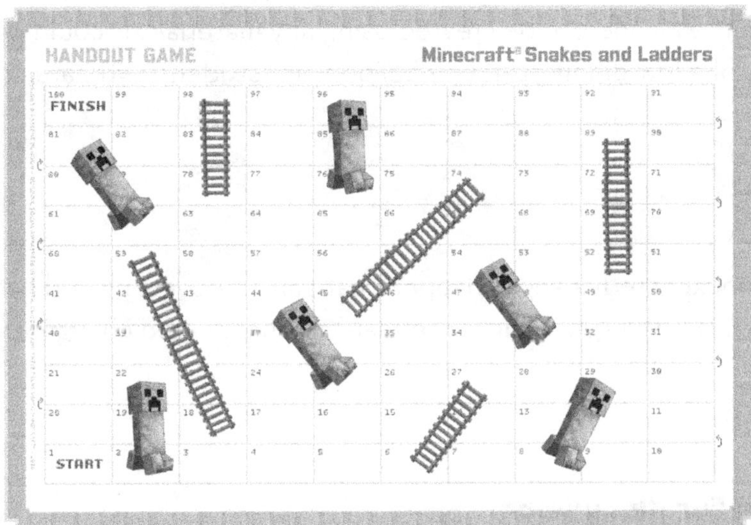

Remember to be a "good sport" whether you win or lose.

How did you feel when you won/lost?

____

____

What did you do at the end of the game to show you were a good sport?

____

____

SESSION 24: MANAGING THE UNEXPECTED

World set-up

For this session, the world should be flat or at least have some flat areas so students can build hot air balloons in an open location.

Minecraft® activity

Students will design and build hot air balloons during this session. These can be built on the ground or in the air and can be created using any materials. It could be helpful to provide pictures of a few different hot air balloons for students who are unsure of what they look like.

Main message

- Sometimes unexpected changes happen that can be upsetting and hard to manage. There are things we can do to manage unexpected changes more effectively.

Key points for discussion

- How do you feel when your plans change unexpectedly?
- Are unexpected changes always in someone's control?
- What can you do to manage unexpected changes when they happen? —refer to handout

Skills to highlight during the session

- Communicating clearly
- Managing unexpected changes effectively
- Helping others

HANDOUT 24 Managing the Unexpected

Session Plan

Time	Activity
5 min	Welcome
10 min	Review Home Challenge
10 min	Managing unexpected changes Talk as a group about how you feel when your plans change unexpectedly: ▪ Disappointed, anxious, angry, sad, confused, etc. Are unexpected changes always in someone's control? e.g. someone is sick, the weather is bad... What can you do to manage unexpected changes when they happen? (see handout)
5 min	Discuss today's activity—building a hot air balloon. Work with partners to discuss materials, features, etc.
10 min	Player 1 builds a hot air balloon
10 min	Player 2 builds a hot air balloon
5 min	Movement break
10 min	Talk to others about what you have built
10 min	Player 1 continues to build or free play
10 min	Player 2 continues to build or free play
5 min	Explain Home Challenge
	Finish

HANDOUT 24 Managing the Unexpected

What we did today

Today we learned about what we can do when changes happen that are unexpected during the following activities:

- With the group, we talked about how we usually feel when something changes unexpectedly. We discussed why we might feel that way and what we can do to help ourselves manage the unexpected changes in a helpful way.
- With our partners, we designed and built hot air balloons in Minecraft®.

- We practiced managing unexpected changes while building in Minecraft® and participating in other activities.

HANDOUT 24 Managing the Unexpected

When an unexpected change happens we can:

Tell ourselves it will be okay

I will be okay.
I can do things differently today.

Use relaxation strategies

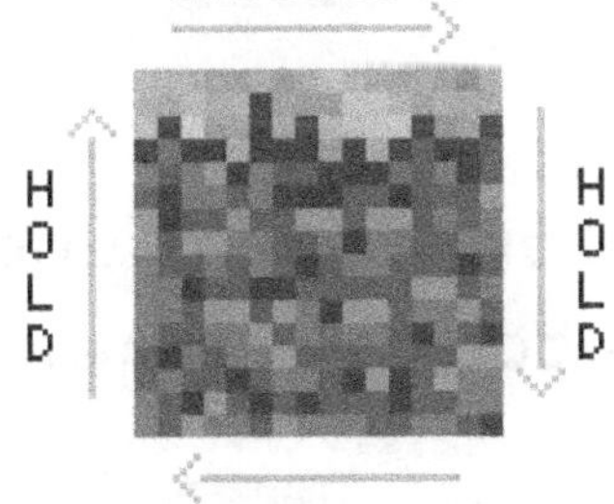

Make a plan

Ask for help

HANDOUT 24 Managing the Unexpected

Home Challenge

Think about how you would feel and what you would do to manage the unexpected changes described below:

You were excited about school sports day, but it got canceled because it was raining.

___

___

It is your best friend's party but you are sick so you have to stay home.

___

___

Your mum said she would take you to the shops after school and buy a new Xbox game, but now she has to work so you can't go.

___

___

SESSION 25: PUTTING IT ALL TOGETHER

SUMMARY SESSION

World set-up

There are no specific requirements for the world for this session, as students can build their underground rollercoasters in any location. Ideally, a world with several different areas or landscapes would be best (e.g. flat area, forest, mountains).

Minecraft® activity

In this session, students will build underground rollercoasters. They will need to find and adapt a cave or dig out a tunnel in the ground to create space to build their rollercoaster. Before going on devices, the group should discuss the features that are important to include in their rollercoasters, and where they could be built.

To construct a rollercoaster, students will need standard rails, powered rails and a minecart from their inventory. Standard rails can be used for any downward parts of the rollercoaster and corners, and powered rails should be used when uphill movement is required.

Main message

- This session is an opportunity to review the content of previous sessions and apply what we have learned.

Key points for discussion

- What is tone of voice?
- How can we figure out the size of a problem and whether we need help to solve it?
- How can we manage unexpected changes effectively?

Skills to highlight during the session

- Noticing the tone of voice of others
- Identifying the size of any problems that occur
- Asking for help when needed
- Being a good sport
- Managing unexpected changes effectively

HANDOUT 25 Putting It All Together

Session Plan

Time	Activity
5 min	Welcome
5 min	Review Home Challenge
10 min	What have we learned about this week? ▪ Tone of voice ▪ Size of the problem ▪ Being a good sport ▪ Managing the unexpected Talk as a group about what we have learned and how we can use this information at school and at home.
5 min	Discuss today's activity—creating an underground rollercoaster. Talk with the group about finding a cave to start building. Discuss materials, placement, etc.
10 min	Player 1 builds an underground rollercoaster
10 min	Player 2 builds an underground rollercoaster
5 min	Movement break
10 min	Discuss what they have created. Was it easy/hard? How did they use the skills they have learned this week?
10 min	Player 1 builds an underground rollercoaster or free play
10 min	Player 2 builds an underground rollercoaster or free play
10 min	Give certificates
	Finish

HANDOUT 25 Putting It All Together

What we did today

Today we reviewed and practiced the skills we have learned over the last few sessions during the following activities:

- With the group, we discussed what we have learned and how we can use these skills at home and at school.

- Working with partners, we made underground rollercoasters in Minecraft® and played some minigames. We had to:
  - Notice how our partners used TONE OF VOICE when talking
  - Consider the SIZE OF THE PROBLEM if things didn't go to plan
  - BE A GOOD SPORT whether we won or lost a game
  - MANAGE UNEXPECTED CHANGES that happened while we were playing.

SESSION 26: WHEN SOMEONE SAYS "NO"

World set-up

There are no specific requirements for the world for this session, as students can build their bridges in any location. Ideally, a world with several different areas or landscapes would be best (e.g. flat area, forest, mountains).

Minecraft® activity

In this session, students will build bridges across the landscape out of any materials that they choose from their inventory. It could be helpful to provide pictures of a few different types of bridges for students who are unsure of what a bridge can look like.

Main message

- Sometimes friends, family or teachers say "no" to us when we ask to have or do something. It can be hard to accept when someone says "no" but there are things we can do to help us manage and feel better.

Key points for discussion

- How do we feel when someone says "no"?
- What are some of the reasons people say "no" when we ask for something?
- What can we do when someone says "no"?

Skills to highlight during the session

- Communicating clearly
- Accepting "no" effectively
- Asking for and accepting help

HANDOUT 26 When Someone Says "No"

Session Plan

Time	Activity
5 min	Welcome
10 min	Group Rules
10 min	When someone says "NO" Talk as a group about how you feel when someone says "NO" to you: ▪ Disappointed, angry, sad, etc. ▪ That it is mean or unfair What are the reasons people say "NO" when you ask for something? ▪ Not a good time ▪ Need to think about the details ▪ Not safe ▪ Not ready What can we do when someone says "NO"?
5 min	Discuss today's activity—building a bridge. Work with partners to discuss materials, features, etc.
10 min	Player 1 builds a bridge
10 min	Player 2 builds a bridge
5 min	Movement break
10 min	Talk to others about what you have built
10 min	Player 1 continues to build or free play
10 min	Player 2 continues to build or free play
5 min	Explain Home Challenge
	Finish

HANDOUT 26 When Someone Says "No"

What we did today

Today we discussed what we can do when someone says "NO" during the following activities:

- With the group, we discussed how we feel when someone says "No." We talked about what we can do to accept someone saying "No" and discussed the reasons people might say "No" to us in different situations.
- With our partners, we designed and built bridges across a river in Minecraft®.

- We practiced considering other possibilities when someone said "No" while building in Minecraft® and participating in other activities.

HANDOUT 26 When Someone Says "No"

What can you do when someone says no?

We can't always do what we want or have what we want when we ask.

Sometimes when we ask the answer is "NO."

When the answer is "NO" we might feel disappointed, angry, sad or something else.

When the answer is "NO" we can name our feeling and why we feel that way.

Then we might try and think of an alternative or a way to feel better.

Remember when someone says "NO" they usually have a good reason, and are not trying to be mean.

HANDOUT 26 When Someone Says "No"

Home Challenge

Think about a time when you really wanted to have or do something and your parents said "NO."

What did you ask for?

____

____

Why did they say "NO"?

____

____

How did you feel?

____

____

What did you do?

____

____

Could you have done something different? What?

____

____

SESSION 27: RESPONDING TO TEASING

World set-up

In this session, the world needs to be flat or feature large open spaces, to enable students to create a giant water tank.

Minecraft® activity

The activity for this session is building a giant fish tank. Students will need to use glass and other materials from their inventory to create a frame and the tank, then use a water bucket to fill the tank with water.

Main message

- Sometimes it can be hard to tell if someone is joking with us in a friendly way or teasing us. If someone teases us, there are a few different things we can do that can help us manage the situation effectively.

Key points for discussion

- What is teasing?
- How do you know if you are being teased?
- How can we tell if someone is teasing us to be mean? —refer to handout
- What can we do if we are being teased? —refer to handout

Skills to highlight during the session

- Communicating clearly
- Being kind

HANDOUT 27 Responding to Teasing

Session Plan

Time	Activity
5 min	Welcome
5 min	Review Group Rules and Home Challenge
10 min	What is teasing? Talk as a group about teasing—what it is, how to tell if someone is teasing you and what to do if you are being teased.
10 min	Discuss today's activity—building a giant fish tank. Talk with the group about what features it will need, what it should be made of, etc.
10 min	Player 1 builds a giant fish tank
10 min	Player 2 builds a giant fish tank
5 min	Movement break
5 min	Discuss what features they have included in their fish tanks. What else would be good to add?
5 min	Talk as a group about their experiences of teasing. Have they been teased? Have they teased others? How does it feel to be teased?
10 min	Player 1 free play
10 min	Player 2 free play
5 min	Explain Home Challenge
	Finish

HANDOUT 27 Responding to Teasing

What we did today

Today we learned about how to respond to teasing during the following activities:

- With the group, we discussed what teasing is, and how we can tell if someone is joking in a friendly way or teasing to be mean.

- Working with partners, we created giant fish tanks in Minecraft®. We had to consider what materials to use and what features to include.
- With the group, we talked about our experiences of being teased and what we can do if someone teases us.

HANDOUT 27 Responding to Teasing

Joking vs teasing

You can tell if someone is joking with you in a friendly way or teasing to be mean by thinking about the following:

- Is the person a friend or family member?

- What tone of voice is the person using?

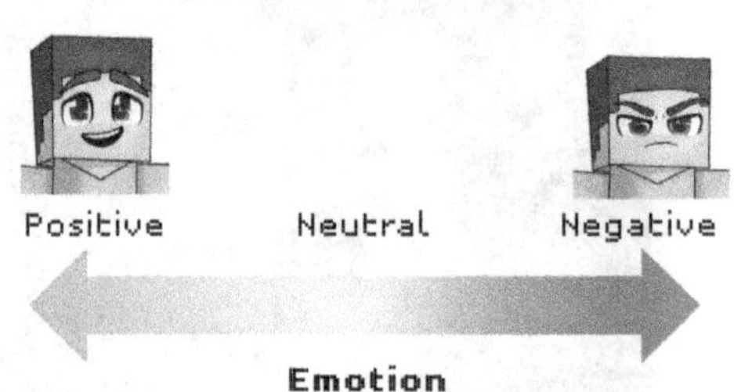

- What does the person's body language tell you?

- What past experiences have you had with the person?

Remember, even if someone is joking with you in a friendly way, you can ask them to stop if it upsets you.

HANDOUT 27 Responding to Teasing

What can we do if we are being teased?
The best thing to do is respond in the way that feels right for you. You could:

Respond like you don't care

Make a joke

Walk away

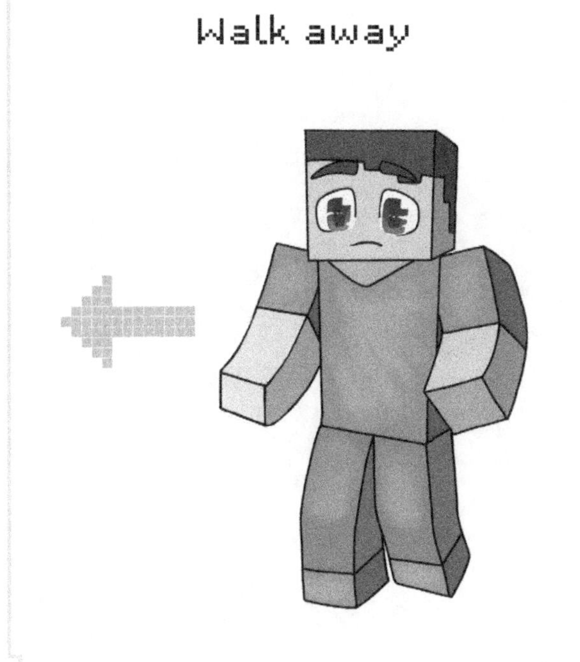

Stand up for yourself

HANDOUT 27 Responding to Teasing

Home Challenge

Imagine your brother is joking with you in a friendly way but you don't like it. How would you respond? (tick the strategies you would use)

- Respond like you don't care
- Make a joke
- Walk away
- Stand up for yourself
- Something else? ______________________

Now imagine you are being teased in a mean way by a bully at school. How would you respond? (tick the strategies you would use)

- Respond like you don't care
- Make a joke
- Walk away
- Stand up for yourself
- Something else? ______________________

SESSION 28: MANAGING DIFFICULT FEELINGS

World set-up

For this session, you will need a desert world with flat ground so students can create a desert temple.

Minecraft® activity

Students will build desert temples during this session. Before going on devices, students will discuss the features of desert temples with the group and then design their temple with partners. When they move to a device, students can use any materials in their inventory to create their temple.

Main message

- All feelings are valid and necessary, but some feelings can be difficult to manage.
- We can learn different ways to help manage difficult feelings when we have them.

Key points for discussion

- What kinds of feelings are difficult to manage? —refer to handout
- How do we know when we are having those feelings?
- What can we do to feel better when we have difficult feelings? —refer to handout

Skills to highlight during the session

- Taking a break to regulate
- Communicating clearly
- Listening to others
- Being kind

HANDOUT 28 Managing Difficult Feelings

Session Plan

Time	Activity
5 min	Welcome
5 min	Review Home Challenge
10 min	Managing difficult feelings Talk as a group about what types of feelings are difficult to manage. How do we know we are having those feelings? What makes us feel that way?
10 min	Discuss today's activity—building a desert temple. Talk with the group about what materials they might use and what it might look like.
5 min	Design and plan a desert temple with partners
10 min	Player 1 builds a desert temple
10 min	Player 2 builds a desert temple
5 min	Movement break
5 min	Discuss what we can do when we experience difficult feelings
10 min	Player 1 finishes desert temple or free play
10 min	Player 2 finishes desert temple or free play
5 min	Explain Home Challenge
	Finish

HANDOUT 28 Managing Difficult Feelings

What we did today

Today we explored how to recognize and manage difficult feelings during the following activities:

- With the group, we discussed what difficult feelings are, when they occur and how we recognize them.

- On devices, we worked with our partners to create desert temples in Minecraft®.
- As a group we discussed what we can do when we are having difficult feelings at school and at home, to help us feel better.

HANDOUT 28 Managing Difficult Feelings

What are difficult feelings?

Difficult feelings could be feelings like:

Anger

Sadness

Frustration

Fear

Worry

How do we recognize difficult feelings?

Thoughts

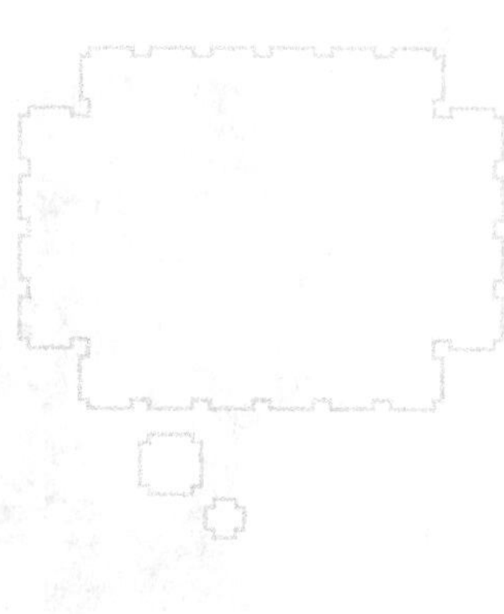

Actions

Physical reactions

HANDOUT 28 Managing Difficult Feelings

How do we manage difficult feelings effectively?

When you battle in Minecraft®, you have armor to protect you and tools to fight your enemy.

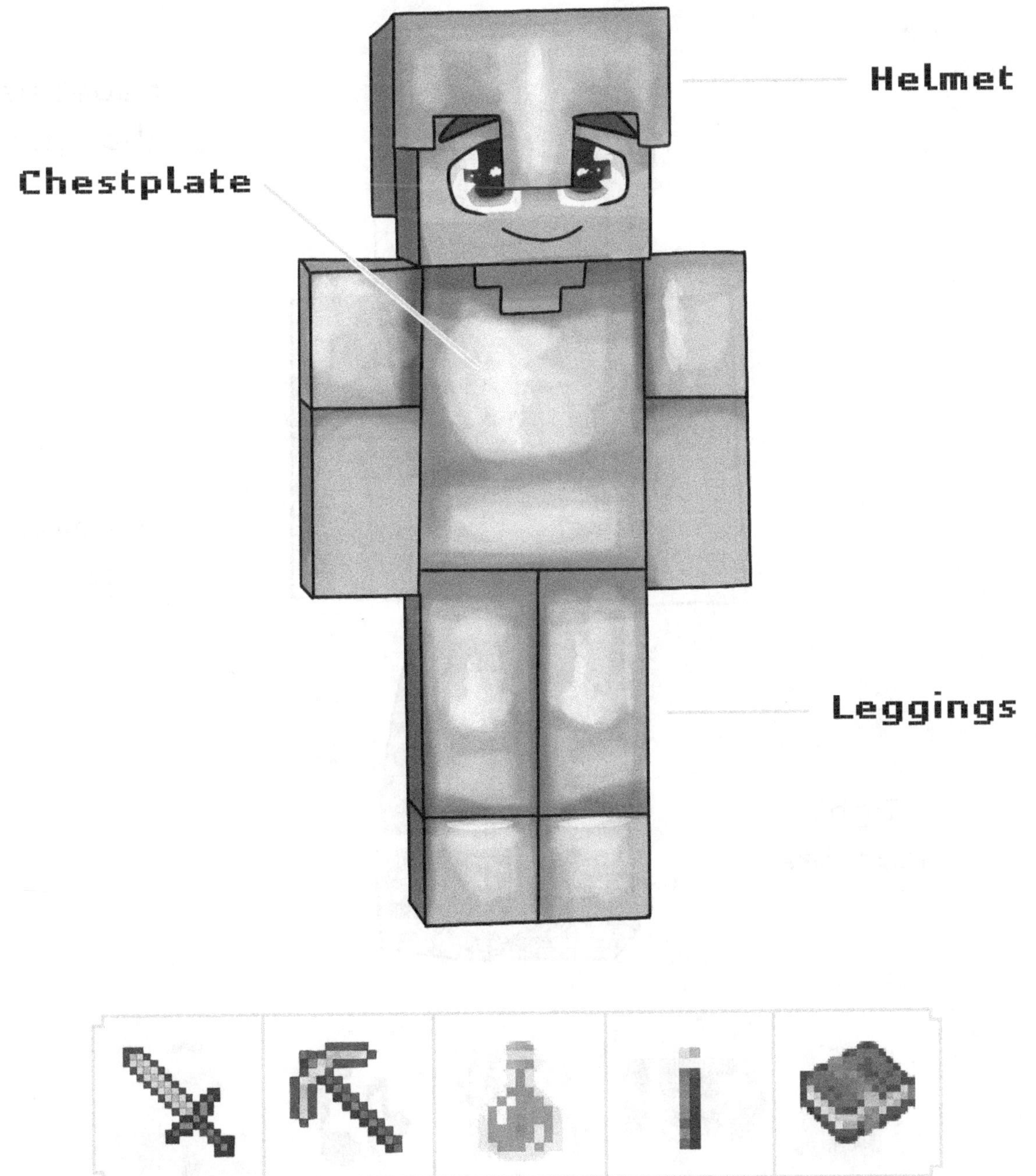

HANDOUT 28 Managing Difficult Feelings

How can you manage difficult feelings effectively?

When you have difficult feelings, you have no armour to protect you, so your feelings go to different parts of your body. You need tools to help you stay safe and feel better.

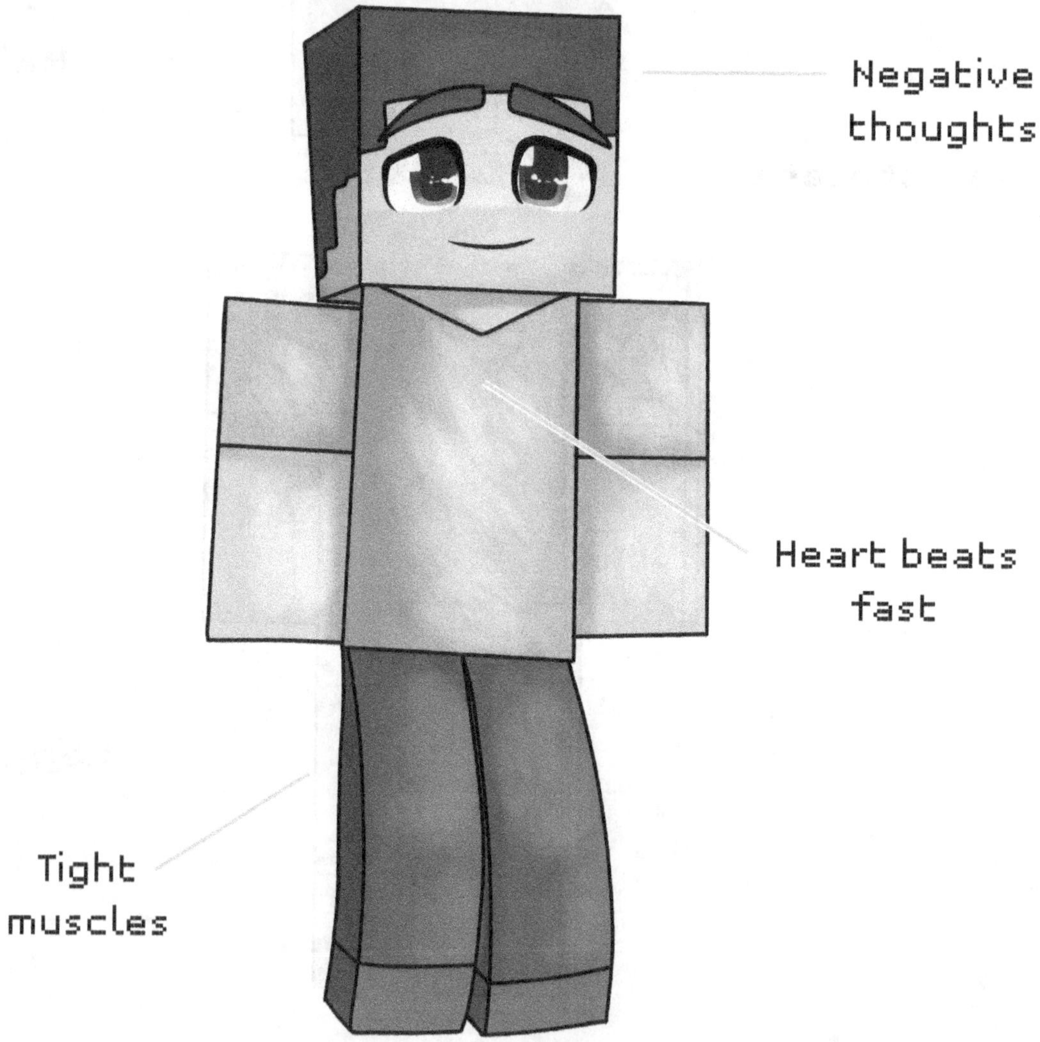

HANDOUT 28 Managing Difficult Feelings

Home Challenge

Fill in the toolbar below to show what tools you use to feel better when you're angry (e.g. deep breaths, taking a break, asking for help, etc.).

Toolbar

SESSION 29: BEING HONEST

World set-up

There are no specific requirements for the world for this session, as students can build their treehouses in any location. Ideally, a world with several different areas or landscapes would be best (e.g. flat area, forest, mountains).

Minecraft® activity

In this session, students will design and build treehouses. As a group, students will discuss what materials to use and features to include in their treehouses. Then they will work on devices to build their treehouses according to their design.

Main message

- Being honest means telling the truth to others. It is important for us to tell the truth to develop trust in relationships.

Key points for discussion

- What is honesty? —refer to handout
- Why is being honest important?
- Why might someone be dishonest or tell a lie?
- What happens when someone is dishonest/doesn't tell the truth?

Skills to highlight during the session

- Helping others
- Being honest
- Communicating clearly
- Being kind

HANDOUT 29 Being Honest

Session Plan

Time	Activity
5 min	Welcome
5 min	Review Home Challenge
10 min	What is honesty? Talk as a group about what honesty is and why it is important. What happens when we are dishonest/don't tell the truth?
10 min	Discuss today's activity—building a treehouse. Talk with the group about finding a place to build. Discuss materials, placement, furniture, etc.
10 min	Player 1 builds treehouse
10 min	Player 2 builds treehouse
5 min	Movement break
10 min	Show treehouses to the group and discuss how they have been built.
10 min	Player 1 continues to build treehouse or free play
10 min	Player 2 continues to build treehouse or free play
5 min	Explain Home Challenge
	Finish

HANDOUT 29 Being Honest

What we did today

Today we discussed why it is important to be honest during the following activities:

- With the group, we used examples to explore honesty, and discussed why we should be honest with others.

- Working with partners, we built treehouses in Minecraft®. We had to design the treehouse, choose materials and find a good place to build.
- With the group, we discussed how we feel and how others feel when we don't tell the truth.

HANDOUT 29 Being Honest

Say what really happened

Tell the whole truth

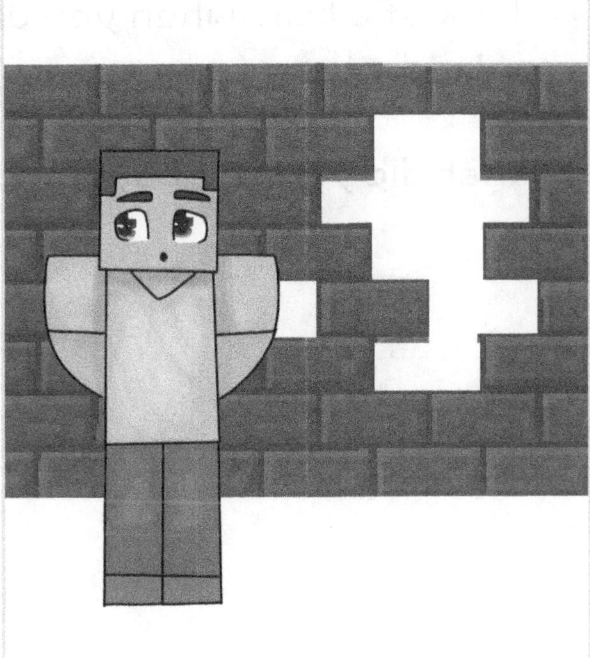

Do what is right

Be honest in your actions

Is this yours?

Home Challenge

Think of a time when you did not tell the truth or told a lie.

What did you lie about?

Why did you lie?

Did anyone find out that you had lied?

How did you feel?

What happened afterwards?

SESSION 30: PUTTING IT ALL TOGETHER

SUMMARY SESSION

World set-up

For this session, the world needs to have plenty of water in which to build pirate ships. An island or a location close to an ocean would be ideal.

Minecraft® activity

In this session, students will design and build their own pirate ships. These can be built at the edge of the shore or in the water and can be created using any materials. It could be helpful to provide pictures of a few different pirate ships for students who are unsure of what a pirate ship can look like.

Main message

- This session is an opportunity to review the content of previous sessions and apply what we have learned.

Key points for discussion

- What can we do if someone says "no" to us?
- How can we tell if someone is teasing to be mean or joking in a friendly way?
- What can we do to feel better when we have difficult feelings?
- Why is it important to always be honest?

Skills to highlight during the session

- Taking a break to stay regulated
- Telling the truth
- Communicating clearly
- Being kind

HANDOUT 30 Putting It All Together

Session Plan

Time	Activity
5 min	Welcome
5 min	Review Home Challenge
10 min	What have we learned about this week? ▪ When someone says "NO" ▪ Responding to teasing ▪ Managing difficult feelings ▪ Being honest Talk as a group about what we have learned and how we can use this information at school and at home.
10 min	Discuss today's activity—building a pirate ship. Decide in pairs what materials are needed, what it will look like, etc.
10 min	Player 1 builds a pirate ship
10 min	Player 2 builds a pirate ship
5 min	Movement break
5 min	Discuss what they have created. Was it easy/hard? Show others what they have made.
10 min	Player 1 builds pirate ship or free play
10 min	Player 2 builds pirate ship or free play
10 min	Give certificates
	Finish

HANDOUT 30 Putting It All Together

What we did today

Today we reviewed and practiced the skills we have learned over the last few sessions during the following activities:

- With the group, we discussed what we have learned and how we can use these skills at home and at school.

- Working with partners, we made pirate ships in Minecraft® and played some minigames.
- With the group, we did a quiz to test our knowledge of the key themes from the last few sessions:
  - WHEN SOMEONE SAYS "NO"
  - RESPONDING TO TEASING
  - MANAGING DIFFICULT FEELINGS
  - BEING HONEST.

SESSION 31: BEING KIND TO OTHERS

World set-up

For this session, you will need a desert world with flat ground so students can create giant sandcastles.

Minecraft® activity

Students will build giant sandcastles during this session. Before going on devices, students will discuss the features of sandcastles with the group and then design their sandcastle with partners. When they move to a device, students can use any materials in their inventory to create their sandcastle.

Main message

- Being kind to others is one way we can show others that we accept them. Being kind is being considerate, caring and accepting towards others without expecting anything in return.

Key points for discussion

- What does it mean to be kind to others and why is it important?
- Do we expect others to be kind to us?
- How do others feel when we are kind to them?
- Is there a benefit to us when we are kind to others?

Skills to highlight during the session

- Helping others
- Telling the truth
- Being kind

HANDOUT 31 Being Kind to Others

Session Plan

Time	Activity
5 min	Welcome
5 min	Discuss and create Group Rules
10 min	Talk as a group about what being kind to others means and why it is important. ▪ What can we do to show kindness to others? ▪ How do others feel when we are kind? ▪ How do you feel when someone is kind to you?
10 min	Discuss today's activity—creating a giant sandcastle
10 min	Player 1 builds a giant sandcastle
10 min	Player 2 builds a giant sandcastle
5 min	Movement break
10 min	Talk to another group member about what your sandcastle looks like and how you built it
10 min	Player 1 continues to build sandcastle or free play
10 min	Player 2 continues to build sandcastle or free play
5 min	Explain Home Challenge
	Finish

HANDOUT 31 Being Kind to Others

What we did today

Today we learned about being kind to others during the following activities:

- With the group, we discussed what being kind to others means and why it is important.
- We considered the following questions:
    - How do others feel when we are kind to them?
    - Is there a benefit to us when we are kind to others?

- With partners, we created giant sandcastles in Minecraft®. We had to consider:
    - Design and shape
    - What features to include
    - Decorations
    - Where to build
    - Materials.

HANDOUT 31 Being Kind to Others

Kindness is being friendly, caring and considerate to others without expecting something in return.

We can be kind to others by:

Listening to their experiences

Helping them with a problem

Accepting them for who they are

Showing you are happy to see them

Showing you care about their feelings

Giving them a compliment

HANDOUT 31 Being Kind to Others

Home Challenge

Think about a time when you were kind to someone then answer the following questions:

Who were you kind to?

How did the person react when you were kind to them?

How did being kind to someone make you feel?

Was it easy or difficult to be kind? Explain.

SESSION 32: BEING RESPONSIBLE FOR YOUR ACTIONS

World set-up

There are no specific requirements for the world for this session, as students can build their fountains in any location. Ideally, a world with some flat or open areas would be best.

Minecraft® activity

In this session, students will design and build fountains. As a group, students will discuss what materials to use and features to include in their fountains. Then they will work on Minecraft® in pairs to build their fountains according to shared or individual designs.

Main message

- Taking responsibility for our actions means being honest and acknowledging when we have said or done something, whether it has had a positive or negative impact.

Key points for discussion

- What does it mean to take responsibility for our actions?
- How can we take responsibility for our actions?
- How do others feel when we apologize?
- How do we feel when someone apologizes to us?

Skills to highlight during the session

- Helping others
- Being kind
- Communicating clearly

HANDOUT 32 Being Responsible for Your Actions

Session Plan

Time	Activity
5 min	Welcome
5 min	Review Home Challenge
10 min	Talk as a group about why it is important to be responsible for our actions. ▪ What does it mean to take responsibility for our actions? ▪ How can we take responsibility for our actions? ▪ How do others feel when we apologize? ▪ How do we feel when someone apologizes to us?
10 min	Discuss today's activity—building a fountain
10 min	Player 1 builds a fountain
10 min	Player 2 builds a fountain
5 min	Movement break
10 min	Talk to another group member about your fountain, materials used, etc.
10 min	Player 1 continues to build a fountain or free play
10 min	Player 2 continues to build a fountain or free play
5 min	Explain Home Challenge
	Finish

HANDOUT 32 Being Responsible for Your Actions

What we did today

Today we learned about being responsible for our actions during the following activities:

- With the group, we discussed why it is important to take responsibility for our actions, even when we have done something by accident. We considered the following questions:
  - How can we take responsibility for our actions?
  - What does it mean to apologize for something we have done?
  - How do others feel when we apologize?
  - How do we feel when someone apologizes to us?

- With partners, we created fountains in Minecraft®. We had to consider:
  - What materials to use
  - What features to include
  - Whether to use water or lava.

HANDOUT 32 Being Responsible for Your Actions

Apologizing means taking responsibility for your words and actions, and letting others know you are sorry if you have hurt them in some way or not done something you said you would.

You might apologize when...

You have hurt someone or their feelings

You have lost or broken something belonging to someone else

You have broken a rule at home or at school

You haven't done something you were supposed to do

NB: You can apologize even if it was an accident.

HANDOUT 32 Being Responsible for Your Actions

When you apologize to someone:

Try to understand how the other person feels

Tell them what you are sorry about

Do or say something to make it right if you can

Don't expect the situation to be instantly better

For example:

- "I'm sorry I hurt your feelings. I won't do it again."
- "I'm sorry I bumped into you. I tripped on the carpet. Are you alright?"
- "I'm sorry I forgot to feed the dog. I'll do it right now."

HANDOUT 32 Being Responsible for Your Actions

Home Challenge

Think about a time when you took responsibility for your actions.

What happened?

____

____

What did you do to take responsibility?

____

____

How did the other person react?

____

____

SESSION 33: GIVING AND ACCEPTING FEEDBACK

World set-up

For this session, the world needs to have plenty of water in which to build houseboats. An island or a location close to an ocean would be ideal.

Minecraft® activity

In this session, students will design and build their own houseboats. These can be built on the surface of the water next to the shore or out in the ocean and can be created using any materials. It could be helpful to provide pictures of a few different houseboats for students who are unsure of what they can look like.

Main message

- Feedback is one way that someone can give us information. Feedback can often help us learn and do things better.

Key points for discussion

- Why is it good to get feedback?
- Is feedback always helpful?
- Who gives us feedback?
- Should we give others feedback? Who? When? Where?
- What can we do when we get feedback from someone?

Skills to highlight during the session

- Giving and accepting feedback
- Being kind
- Communicating clearly

HANDOUT 33 Giving and Accepting Feedback

Session Plan

Time	Activity
5 min	Welcome
5 min	Review Group Rules and Home Challenge
10 min	Talk as a group about what feedback is and what we might get feedback about at home and at school. ▪ Why is it good to get feedback? ▪ Is feedback always helpful? ▪ Who gives us feedback? ▪ Should we give others feedback? Who? When? Where? ▪ What can we do when we get feedback from someone?
10 min	Discuss today's activity—building a houseboat
10 min	Player 1 builds a houseboat
10 min	Player 2 builds a houseboat
5 min	Movement break
10 min	Talk to another group member about what your houseboat looks like and how you built it
10 min	Player 1 continues to build houseboat or free play
10 min	Player 2 continues to build houseboat or free play
5 min	Explain Home Challenge
	Finish

HANDOUT 33 Giving and Accepting Feedback

What we did today

Today we learned about giving and accepting feedback during the following activities:

- With the group, we discussed what feedback is and how accepting helpful feedback can assist us to improve our skills. We considered the following questions:
  - Why do teachers and parents give us feedback?
  - How do we feel when we are given feedback?
  - What can we do when we are given feedback?
  - When should we give feedback to others?

- With partners, we created houseboats in Minecraft®. We had to consider:
  - Design and shape
  - What features to include
  - Where to build
  - Materials.
- We practiced giving and accepting feedback while building our houseboats.

HANDOUT 33 Giving and Accepting Feedback

Feedback is just information

Feedback can be positive, constructive or negative

Positive feedback tells you what you are doing well

Constructive feedback focuses on what you can do differently or better

Negative feedback focuses on what you did wrong or what someone didn't like about what you did

HANDOUT 33 Giving and Accepting Feedback

When someone gives you feedback it can be helpful to...

Listen to what they say

Try to stay calm

Ask questions to help you understand

Thank them for the feedback

Think—was the feedback helpful?

HANDOUT 33 Giving and Accepting Feedback

Home Challenge

Think about a time when a parent or teacher gave you feedback and then answer the following questions.

What were you doing?

What feedback did they give you?

Was the feedback helpful?

How did you react?

SESSION 34: LEARNING FROM MISTAKES

World set-up

For this session, the world should be flat or at least have some flat areas so students can build 3D food in an open location.

Minecraft® activity

Students will design and build 3D versions of their favorite foods during this session. These can be created using any materials. It could be helpful to provide pictures of some different foods created in Minecraf® for students who may be unsure of how to get started.

Main message

- Everyone makes mistakes, but sometimes it can feel really upsetting when we make a mistake. Mistakes can actually help us learn and improve.

Key points for discussion

- How do you feel when you make a mistake?
- Can making mistakes be helpful?
- What can we do when we make a mistake?

Skills to highlight during the session

- Helping others
- Communicating clearly
- Being kind

HANDOUT 34 Learning from Mistakes

Session Plan

Time	Activity
5 min	Welcome
5 min	Review Group Rules and Home Challenge
10 min	Talk as a group about what a mistake is and how we can learn from our mistakes. ▪ How do you feel when you make a mistake? ▪ Can making mistakes be helpful? ▪ What can we do when we make a mistake?
10 min	Discuss today's activity—building a 3D version of your favorite food
10 min	Player 1 builds 3D food
10 min	Player 2 builds 3D food
5 min	Movement break
10 min	Talk to another group member about what food you built and how you built it
10 min	Player 1 continues to build 3D food or free play
10 min	Player 2 continues to build 3D food or free play
5 min	Explain Home Challenge
	Finish

HANDOUT 34 Learning from Mistakes

What we did today

Today we learned about making mistakes and how we can learn from them during the following activities:

- With the group, we discussed what kinds of mistakes we might make at home, at school or out in the community. We discussed the fact that everyone makes mistakes and how making mistakes can help us learn and develop. We considered the following questions:
    - Why do mistakes happen?
    - How do we feel when we make a mistake?
    - How can mistakes help us learn?
    - What can we do when we make a mistake?
- With partners, we created 3D pixel art versions of our favourite foods in Minecraft®. We had to consider:
    - What to make
    - What features to include
    - What materials to use.

- We practiced learning from our mistakes while creating our food pixel art.

HANDOUT 34 Learning from Mistakes

When you make a mistake you can...

Take a break or some deep breaths

Find the reason for the mistake

Try to fix it if you can

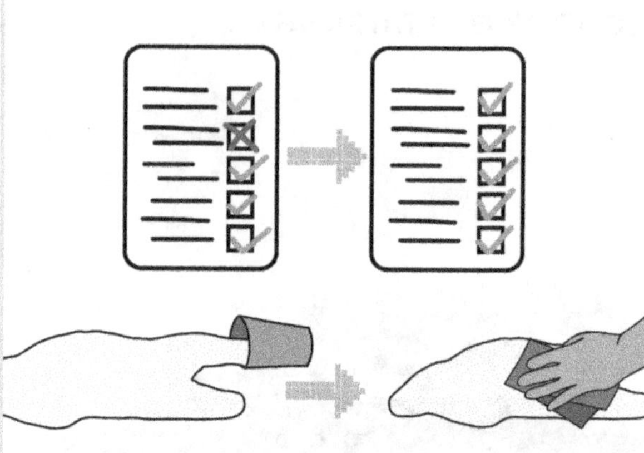

Ask for help

Think—can I learn from this?

HANDOUT 34 Learning from Mistakes

Mistakes might happen when we...

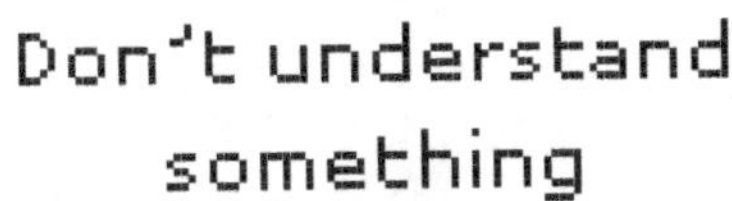

Don't understand something

Get distracted

Are rushing

Are trying something new

HANDOUT 34 Learning from Mistakes

Home Challenge

Imagine you have made each of the mistakes below and answer the following questions.

- How could you fix the mistake?
- What could you learn from the mistake?

You spilled your drink on the table.

____

____

You made a spelling mistake on your writing at school.

____

____

You were playing with your brother's toy and you broke it.

____

____

You used the wrong color on an art project.

____

____

SESSION 35: PUTTING IT ALL TOGETHER

SUMMARY SESSION

World set-up

For this session, the world should be flat or at least have some flat areas so students can build a campsite in an open location.

Minecraft® activity

In this session, students will design and build their own campsites. These can be built in a forest, in the mountains or on the shore of a river or the ocean and can be created using any materials. As a group, students can discuss the important elements to include in their campsites before moving to devices.

Main message

- This session is an opportunity to review the content of previous sessions and apply what we have learned.

Key points for discussion

- What does it mean to be kind to others?
- Why should we take responsibility for our actions?
- How can feedback be helpful?
- How can we learn from our mistakes?

Skills to highlight during the session

- Being kind
- Taking responsibility and learning from mistakes
- Communicating clearly
- Helping others

HANDOUT 35 Putting It All Together

Session Plan

Time	Activity
5 min	Welcome
5 min	Review Home Challenge
10 min	Talk as a group about the topics we have discussed this week. What have you learned? ▪ Being kind to others ▪ Giving and accepting feedback ▪ Learning from mistakes ▪ Taking responsibility for our actions
10 min	Discuss today's activity—building a campsite/caravan
10 min	Player 1 builds a campsite/caravan
10 min	Player 2 builds a campsite/caravan
5 min	Movement break
10 min	Talk to another group member about your campsite/caravan, materials used, etc.
10 min	Player 1 continues to build a campsite/caravan or free play
10 min	Player 2 continues to build a campsite/caravan or free play
5 min	Give certificates
	Finish

HANDOUT 35 Putting It All Together

What we did today

Today we reviewed and practiced the skills we have learned over the last few sessions during the following activities:

- With the group, we discussed what we have learned and how we can use these skills at home and at school.

- Working in pairs, we made campsites in Minecraft®. We had to:
  - Be KIND to the members of the group
  - Stay calm and learn from our MISTAKES
  - GIVE and ACCEPT FEEDBACK
  - TAKE RESPONSIBILITY if we did something to upset someone.

SESSION 36: CONNECTING WITH OTHERS

World set-up

For this session, the world needs to have plenty of water in which to build underwater houses. An island or a location close to an ocean would be ideal.

Minecraft® activity

In this session, students will design and build their own underwater houses. These can be built in the water next to the shore or out in the ocean and can be created using any materials. Students should discuss the features and materials required with their partners and find suitable locations for them to build separately or together before going onto Minecraft®.

Main message

- There are many different ways that we can spend time with and connect with others.

Key points for discussion

- When might we want to connect with others?
- What does this look like for you (e.g. a conversation, game, activity, online)?
- Do you prefer to connect in person or online or in some other way?

Skills to highlight during the session

- Communicating clearly
- Being kind
- Listening to others

HANDOUT 36 Connecting with Others

Session Plan

Time	Activity
5 min	Welcome
10 min	Group Rules
10 min	Connecting with others Talk as a group about when we might want to connect with others and what this might look like (e.g. a conversation, game, activity).
5 min	Discuss today's activity—creating an underwater house. Talk with the group about what you need to consider before you start building. Discuss materials, placement, etc.
10 min	Player 1 builds an underwater house
10 min	Player 2 builds an underwater house
5 min	Movement break
10 min	How can we connect with others? Do you prefer to connect in person, online or another way?
10 min	Player 1 continues to build underwater house or free play
10 min	Player 2 continues to build underwater house or free play
5 min	Explain Home Challenge
	Finish

HANDOUT 36 Connecting with Others

What we did today

Today we explored how we can connect with others during the following activities:

- With the group, we discussed when we might want to connect with others, and the different ways we can do this.
- Then we talked about what we can do if we would like to connect with others.

- Working with partners, we designed and built underwater houses in Minecraft®. We had to consider:
  - Where to build
  - What materials to use
  - What features to include.

HANDOUT 36 Connecting with Others

There are many different ways that you can connect with others including:

Playing games

Playing

Having a conversation

Playing together online

Hanging out

Eating together

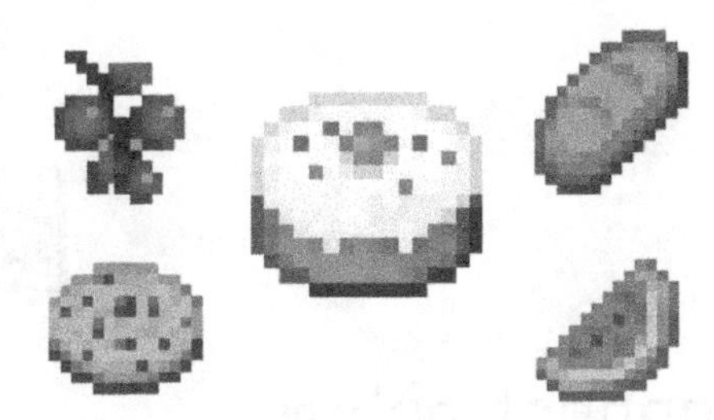

Joining a club

Working together

HANDOUT 36 Connecting with Others

When you want to connect with others you could:

Ask if you can join in

Send a text, email or meme

Talk on the phone

Connect online

HANDOUT 36 Connecting with Others

Home Challenge

Think about a time when you connected with others:

Who did you connect with (e.g. family, friends, etc.)?

What did you do?

How did you feel?

SESSION 37: RESPECTING AND SETTING BOUNDARIES

World set-up

There are no specific requirements for the world for this session, as students can build their fountains in any location. Ideally, a world with several different areas or landscapes would be best (e.g. flat area, forest, mountains).

Minecraft® activity

In this session, students will design and build fountains. As a group, students will discuss what materials to use and features to include in their fountains, as well as deciding whether to use water or lava in their fountain. Then they will work on devices in pairs to build their fountains according to their design.

Main message

- It is important to be able to set boundaries with others to make sure we feel safe and comfortable and can live according to our beliefs and preferences.
- We should accept others' boundaries just like we want others to respect ours.

Key points for discussion

- What do we mean by personal boundaries?
- Why is it important to respect others' boundaries and also be clear about our own boundaries?
- What boundaries do you set with friends and family?
- How do you feel when someone doesn't respect your boundaries?
- How do you communicate your boundaries to others?

Skills to highlight during the session

- Communicating clearly
- Being assertive
- Respecting boundaries
- Being kind

HANDOUT 37 Respecting and Setting Boundaries

Session Plan

Time	Activity
5 min	Welcome
10 min	Review Home Challenge
10 min	Respecting and setting boundaries Talk as a group about what we mean by personal boundaries and why it is important to respect others' boundaries and also be clear about our own boundaries. ▪ What boundaries do you set with friends and family? ▪ How do you feel when someone doesn't respect your boundaries? ▪ How do you communicate your boundaries to others?
5 min	Discuss today's activity—building a secret hideout behind a waterfall. Work with partners to discuss materials, features, etc.
10 min	Player 1 builds secret hideout
10 min	Player 2 builds secret hideout
5 min	Movement break
10 min	Talk to others about what you have built
10 min	Player 1 continues to build or free play
10 min	Player 2 continues to build or free play
5 min	Explain Home Challenge
	Finish

HANDOUT 37 Respecting and Setting Boundaries

What we did today

Today we learned about respecting and setting boundaries during the following activities:

- With the group, we discussed what we mean by personal boundaries and why it is important to respect others' boundaries and also be clear about our own boundaries.
- We talked about what we might have boundaries for including physical touch and sharing of personal information, and explored our right to say "No" when someone tries to pressure us to do something we are not comfortable with.

- With our partners, we designed and built secret hideouts behind waterfalls in Minecraft®.

HANDOUT 37 Respecting and Setting Boundaries

Personal boundaries are limits we set to help us stay happy and safe.

Some examples of how to communicate personal boundaries could be:

"Please don't touch my pencil case without asking."

"No, I don't share my lunch."

"I'm not comfortable talking about that."

"I don't talk about people behind their back."

"Sorry, I don't like hugs."

"Sorry, I can only stay for an hour and then I will need a break."

HANDOUT 37 Respecting and Setting Boundaries

Home Challenge

We all have different personal boundaries. How do you feel about the following situations?

Your grandma wants to kiss you when she greets you. Would you feel comfortable or set a boundary?

Your friend wants to borrow money from you for the canteen. Would you feel comfortable or set a boundary?

Your friend keeps taking your eraser in class without asking. Would you feel comfortable or set a boundary?

SESSION 38: LISTENING TO YOUR BODY

World set-up

For this session, the world needs to have a coastline on which to build lighthouses. An island or a location close to an ocean would be ideal. Alternatively, students could create their own island to then build a lighthouse.

Minecraft® activity

In this session, students will design and build lighthouses. As a group or in pairs, students will discuss what materials to use and features to include in their lighthouses. Then they will work on the devices in pairs to build their lighthouses according to their design.

Main message

- Interoception is a body sense that gives us messages about internal states like hunger, thirst, pain and emotions.
- Sometimes these messages are loud, quiet or even confusing.
- Being aware of these messages can help us understand our needs better.

Key points for discussion

- What is interoception and what can it tell us? —refer to handout
- Messages can be loud (e.g. obvious and possibly overwhelming), quiet (difficult to notice) or confusing (unclear what they mean).
- How do you experience messages from your body?
- What do different body sensations mean for you? (e.g. tummy rumbling could mean we are hungry, etc.)

Skills to highlight during the session

- Communicating clearly
- Noticing when we need a break to regulate
- Being kind
- Asking for and accepting help

HANDOUT 38 Listening to Your Body

Session Plan

Time	Activity
5 min	Welcome
10 min	Review Home Challenge
10 min	Listening to your body With the group, discuss what interoception is and what it can tell us. (see handout) Talk about interoception in terms of messages being loud (e.g. obvious and possibly overwhelming), quiet (difficult to notice) or confusing (unclear what they mean) and ask the group what their experiences are.
5 min	Discuss today's activity—creating a lighthouse. Talk with the group about what you need to consider before you start building. Discuss materials, placement, etc.
10 min	Player 1 builds a lighthouse
10 min	Player 2 builds a lighthouse
5 min	Movement break
10 min	Share examples of different body sensations and what they might mean (e.g. tummy rumbling could mean we are hungry, etc.)
10 min	Player 1 continues to build a lighthouse or free play
10 min	Player 2 continues to build a lighthouse or free play
5 min	Explain Home Challenge
	Finish

HANDOUT 38 Listening to Your Body

What we did today

Today we explored how we can listen to our bodies to understand how we feel and what we need during the following activities:

- With the group, we discussed interoception, our body's internal messaging system, and what it can tell us.
- Then we talked about whether our body's signals are loud, quiet or confusing, and what particular sensations in our bodies might be telling us.

- Working with partners, we designed and built lighthouses in Minecraft®. We had to consider:
  - Where to build
  - What materials to use
  - What features to include
  - How tall it should be.

HANDOUT 38 Listening to Your Body

Interoception is an internal body sense that can send messages to us about:

Hunger or fullness

Thirst

Sickness or pain

Needing the toilet

Body temperature

Tiredness

Emotions

Stress or arousal

HANDOUT 38 Listening to Your Body

Home Challenge

Think about the messages your body sends you.
How does your body let you know that you are...

Hungry?

Tired?

Angry?

SESSION 39: RESPECTING PERSONAL SPACE

World set-up

There are no specific requirements for the world for this session, as students can build their floating islands in the sky in any location. Ideally, a world with several different areas or landscapes would be best (e.g. flat area, forest, mountains).

Minecraft® activity

In this session, students will design and build floating islands. As a group, students will discuss what materials to use and features to include in their floating islands. Then they will work on devices in pairs to build their floating islands, incorporating their ideas. To make an island float in the sky, students will first need to build a tower of single blocks to the height they want, then build their island on top of it. Once their island is finished, they can destroy the blocks of the tower and the island will float.

Main message

- Personal space is the amount of space we need around our bodies to feel comfortable.
- We all have different sized personal space bubbles, and they can get bigger or smaller depending on where we are and who we are with.
- It is important to respect the personal space of others and communicate our own needs regarding personal space.

Key points for discussion

- What is personal space and why is it important to respect the personal space of others? —refer to handout
- How can you respect the personal space of others?
- How do you feel when others invade your personal space?
- How can you let others know your needs about personal space?

Skills to highlight during the session

- Respecting the personal space of others
- Communicating personal space needs clearly
- Being kind
- Listening to others

HANDOUT 39 Respecting Personal Space

Session Plan

Time	Activity
5 min	Welcome
10 min	Review Home Challenge
10 min	Respecting personal space Talk as a group about what personal space is and why it is important to respect the personal space of others. How can you respect the personal space of others? How far away from someone should you be when you are having a conversation, sitting on the mat, etc.? How do you feel when others invade your personal space? How do others react if you invade their personal space bubble?
5 min	Discuss today's activity—building a floating island. Work with partners to discuss materials, features, etc.
10 min	Player 1 creates a floating island
10 min	Player 2 creates a floating island
5 min	Movement break
5 min	Talk to others about what you have built
5 min	What can you do if someone invades your personal space? What if you need to invade someone's personal space to get something or go somewhere?
10 min	Player 1 continues to build or free play
10 min	Player 2 continues to build or free play
5 min	Explain Home Challenge
	Finish

HANDOUT 39 Respecting Personal Space

What we did today

Today we learned about respecting personal space during the following activities:

- With the group, we discussed what personal space is and why it is important to be aware of personal space when we are with others. We also talked about how we feel when others invade our personal space and how others might react when we invade theirs.
- With our partners, we designed and built floating islands in Minecraft®.

- We practiced respecting the personal space of others while building in Minecraft® and participating in other activities.

HANDOUT 39 Respecting Personal Space

Personal space is the amount of space we need around our bodies to feel comfortable.

Everyone has a personal space bubble surrounding them

Your personal space bubble might get bigger or smaller depending on who you are with and what you are doing

People feel uncomfortable when you invade their personal space bubble without permission

Always ask for permission before touching someone or giving someone a hug

Try to leave an arm's length between you and the person you are talking to or standing with

HANDOUT 39 Respecting Personal Space

Home Challenge

Thinking about your personal space bubble, draw yourself in the following situations making sure you leave enough space between you and the people around you.

SESSION 40: PUTTING IT ALL TOGETHER

SUMMARY SESSION

World set-up

For this session, the world should be flat or at least have some flat areas and lots of open sky so students can build UFOs in an open location.

Minecraft® activity

In this session, students will design and build their own UFOs. These can be built on the ground or in the air and can be created using any materials. It could be helpful to provide pictures of a few different UFOs for students who are unsure of what a UFO can look like.

Main message

- This session is an opportunity to review the content of previous sessions and apply what we have learned.

Key points for discussion

- How do you like to connect with others?
- What messages does your body give you to help you understand how you feel and what you need?
- Why is it important to have personal boundaries and respect the boundaries of others?
- What is personal space?

Skills to highlight during the session

- Connecting through Minecraft®
- Respecting personal boundaries
- Being aware of personal space
- Noticing when we need a break to regulate
- Communicating clearly
- Being kind

HANDOUT 40 Putting It All Together

Session Plan

Time	Activity
5 min	Welcome
10 min	Review Home Challenge
10 min	What have we learned about this week? ▪ Connecting with others ▪ Respecting and setting boundaries ▪ Listening to your body ▪ Respecting personal space Talk as a group about what we have learned and how we can use this information at school and at home.
5 min	Discuss today's activity—building a UFO. Work with partners to discuss materials, features, etc.
10 min	Player 1 builds a UFO
10 min	Player 2 builds a UFO
5 min	Movement break
10 min	Talk to others about what you have built
10 min	Player 1 continues to build or free play
10 min	Player 2 continues to build or free play
5 min	Give certificates
	Finish

HANDOUT 40 Putting It All Together

What we did today

Today we reviewed and practiced the skills we have learned over the last few sessions during the following activities:

- With the group, we discussed what we have learned and how we can use these skills at home and at school.
- With our partners, we designed and built UFOs in Minecraft®.

- While we worked on Minecraft®, we considered the key themes from the last few sessions:
  - CONNECTING WITH OTHERS
  - RESPECTING AND SETTING BOUNDARIES
  - LISTENING TO YOUR BODY
  - RESPECTING PERSONAL SPACE.

PART 3
Resources

HANDOUT GAME

Minecraft® Snakes and Ladders

100 FINISH	99	98	97	96	95	94	93	92	91
81	82	83	84	85	86	87	88	89	90
80	[illegible]	78	77	76	75	74	73	72	71
61	[illegible]	63	64	65	66	[illegible]	68	69	70
60	59	58	57	56	[illegible]	54	53	52	51
41	42	43	44	45	46	47	[illegible]	49	50
40	39	[illegible]	37	[illegible]	35	34	[illegible]	32	31
21	22	[illegible]	24	[illegible]	26	27	28	29	30
20	19	18	17	16	15	[illegible]	13	[illegible]	11
1 START	2	3	4	5	6	7	8	9	10

CERTIFICATES of Completion

Congratulations!

This certificate recognizes

____

for successfully completing the Minecraft® Social Group

Presented by: ____________________

Date: ____________________

Congratulations!

This certificate recognizes

____

for successfully completing the Minecraft® Social Group

Presented by: ____________________

Date: ____________________

Congratulations!

This certificate recognizes

____

for successfully completing the Minecraft® Social Group

Presented by: ____________________

Date: ____________________

Congratulations!

This certificate recognizes

for successfully completing the Minecraft® Social Group

Presented by:

Date:

Congratulations!

This certificate recognizes

for successfully completing the Minecraft® Social Group

Presented by:

Date:

Helpful Websites

MINECRAFT

Minecraft Official Website
https://minecraft.net

Minecraft Wiki
https://minecraft.fandom.com/wiki/Minecraft_Wiki

Minecraft Crafting Recipes
www.minecraft-crafting.net

Minecraft 101
www.minecraft101.net/index.html

NEURODIVERSITY-AFFIRMING PRACTICE

Reframing Autism
https://reframingautism.org.au

Autistic Self Advocacy Network
https://autisticadvocacy.org

Studio 3—The Low Arousal Approach
www.studio3.org/training-and-coaching/low-arousal-training

Bibliography

Anketell, C., Rose, R. (2009) The benefits of social skills groups for young people with autism spectrum disorder: A pilot study. *Child Care in Practice* 15, 2, 127–144.

Baron-Cohen, S., Gomez De La Cuesta, G., Krauss, G.W., LeGoff, D.B. (2014) *LEGO®-Based Therapy: How to Build Social Competence Through LEGO®-Based Clubs for Children with Autism and Related Conditions.* London: Jessica Kingsley Publishers.

Bernard-Opitz, V., Sriram, N., Nakhoda-Sapuan, S. (2001) Enhancing social problem solving in children with autism and normal children through computer-assisted instruction. *Journal of Autism and Developmental Disorders* 31, 4, 377–384.

Botha, M., Dibb, B., Frost, D.M. (2022) "It's being a part of a grand tradition, a grand counter-culture which involves communities": A qualitative investigation of autistic community connectedness. *Autism: The International Journal of Research and Practice* 26, 8, 2151–2164.

Bowlby, M. (2023) Creating a neuro-affirming classroom for early childhood. Accessed on 17 April 2025 at https://aane.org/autism-info-faqs/library/creating-a-neuro-affirming-classroom-for-early-childhood

Carpendale, J., Lewis, C. (2006) *How Children Develop Social Understanding.* Malden: Blackwell Publishing.

Clifford Scheflen, C. (2009) *Video Modeling to Teach Play (Language and Social Skills) to Children with Autism.* Presented at the USAAA 2009 Conference in Los Angeles, California.

Cook, J. (2011) *The Worst Day of My Life Ever!* Boys Town, NE: Boys Town Press.

Cook, J. (2012) *Sorry I Forgot to Ask!* Boys Town, NE: Boys Town Press.

Cook, J. (2012) *Team Work Isn't My Thing and I Don't Like to Share!* Boys Town, NE: Boys Town Press.

Cook, J. (2013) *I Just Want to Do It My Way!* Boys Town, NE: Boys Town Press.

Cook, J. (2013) *Thanks for the Feedback, I Think.* Boys Town, NE: Boys Town Press.

Cook, J. (2014) *I Can't Believe You Said That!* Boys Town, NE: Boys Town Press.

Cook, J. (2015) *But It's Not My Fault!* Boys Town, NE: Boys Town Press.

Cook, J. (2016) *That Rule Doesn't Apply to Me!* Boys Town, NE: Boys Town Press.

Cordeiro, A., Nelson, E. (2015) *Minecraft Construction for Dummies, Portable Edition.* Hoboken, NJ: John Wiley & Sons Inc.

Cordeiro, J. (2015) *Minecraft Redstone for Dummies, Portable Edition.* Hoboken, NJ: John Wiley & Sons Inc.

Crompton, C.J., Ropar, D., Evans-Williams, C.V., Flynn, E.G., Fletcher-Watson, S. (2020) Autistic peer-to-peer information transfer is highly effective. *Autism* 24, 7, 1704–1712.

Dallman, A.R., Williams, K.L., Villa, L. (2022) Neurodiversity-affirming practices are a moral imperative for occupational therapy. *The Open Journal of Occupational Therapy* 10, 2, 1–9.

Dekker, V., Nauta, M.H., Mulder, E.J., Timmerman, M.E., de Bildt, A. (2014) A randomized controlled study of a social skills training for preadolescent children with autism spectrum disorders: Generalization of skills by training parents and teachers? *BMC Psychiatry* 14, 189. Accessed on 17 April 2025 at www.biomedcentral.com/1471-244X/14/189

Dekker, M. (1999) *On our own terms: Emerging autistic culture.* Autism99 online conference. Accessed on 17 April 2025 at www.autscape.org/2015/programme/handouts/Autistic-Culture-07-Oct-1999.pdf.

Delahooke, M. (2019) *Beyond Behaviors: Using Brain Science and Compassion to Understand and Solve Children's Behavioral Challenges.* Eau Claire, WI: Pesi Inc.

den Houting, J. (2019) Why Everything You Know About Autism Is Wrong. TEDx. Accessed on 17 April 2025 at www.ted.com/talks/jac_den_

houting_why_everything_you_know_about_autism_is_wrong?language=en

Dundon, R. (2023) *The Therapists' Guide to Neurodiversity Affirming Practice with Children and Young People.* London: Jessica Kingsley Publishers.

Elven, B., Wiman, T. (2017) *Sulky, Rowdy, Rude?: Why Kids Really Act Out and What to Do About It.* London: Jessica Kingsley Publishers.

Enright, J. (2022) Communication Differences and not Deficits. Medium. Accessed on 17 April 2025 at https://medium.com/neurodiversified/cultural-and-communication-differences-f87158533c04

Farwell, N. (2015) *Minecraft: Redstone Handbook (Updated Edition): An Official Mojang Book.* New York: Scholastic Inc.

Gaddy, C., Crow, H. (2023) A primer on neurodiversity-affirming speech and language services for autistic individuals. *Perspectives of the ASHA Special Interest Groups 8*, 6, 1220–1233.

Goodall, E., Brownlow, C. (2022) *Interoception and Regulation: Teaching Skills of Body Awareness and Supporting Connection with Others.* London: Jessica Kingsley Publishers.

Graves, S. (2012) *Hippo Owns Up.* London: Hachette Kids Franklin Watts.

Graves, S. (2016) *Elephant Learns to Share.* London: Windmill Books.

Graves, S. (2016) *Monkey Needs to Listen.* London: Hachette Kids Franklin Watts.

Greene, R. (2011) *The Explosive Child.* London: Harper Collins Publishers Ltd.

Harper, C.B., Symon, J.B.G., Frea, W.D. (2008) Recess is time-in: Using peers to improve social skills of children with autism. *Journal of Autism and Developmental Disorders 38*, 815.

Jones, S., Brush, K., Bailey, R., Brion-Meisels, G. *et al.* (2017) *Navigating SEL from the Inside Out: Looking Inside & Across 25 Leading SEL Programs: A Practical Resource for Schools and OST Providers.* The Wallace Foundation. Accessed on 17 April 2025 at www.wallacefoundation.org/knowledge-center/Documents/Navigating-Social-and-Emotional-Learning-from-the-Inside-Out.pdf

Kasari, C., Rotheram-Fuller, E., Locke, J., Gulsrud, A. (2012) Making the connection: Randomized controlled trial of social skills at school for children with autism spectrum disorders. *The Journal of Child Psychology and Psychiatry 53*, 4, 431–439.

Keating, J., Hashmi, S., Vanderwert, R.E., Davies, R.M., Jones, C.R.G., Gerson, S.A. (2023) Embracing neurodiversity in doll play: Investigating neural and language correlates of doll play in a neurodiverse sample. *European Journal of Neuroscience*, 1–18.

Koegel, R.L., Kern Koegel, L., Oliver, K. (2016) *Using a Child's Restricted Interests to Increase Social Inclusion.* Organization for Autism Research. Accessed on 17 April 2025 at https://researchautism.org/using-a-childs-restricted-interest-to-increase-social-inclusion

leonardoyeates (2019) Autistic communication differences and how to adjust for them. Neuroclastic. Accessed on 17 April 2025 at https://neuroclastic.com/autism-autistic-communication-differences

LeGroff, D.B. (2017) *How LEGO®-Based Therapy for Autism Works: Landing on My Planet.* London: Jessica Kingsley Publishers.

McDonnell, A. (2019) *The Reflective Journey: A Practitioner's Guide to the Low Arousal Approach.* Alcester: Studio3.

Meadows, C. (2017) *Understanding Child Development: Psychological Perspectives and Applications.* London: Taylor & Francis Ltd.

Milton, D.E.M. (2012) On the ontological status of autism: The "double empathy problem." *Disability and Society 27*, 6, 883–887.

Mojang AB (2015) *Minecraft: Beginner's Handbook—Updated Edition: An Official Minecraft Book from Mojang.* London: Egmont UK Ltd.

Mojang AB (2017) *Minecraft Guide to Creative: An Official Minecraft Book from Mojang.* London: Egmont Childrens Books.

Morrison, K.E., DeBrabander, K.M., Jones, D.R., Faso, D.J., Ackerman, R.A., Sasson, N.J. (2020) Outcomes of real-world social interaction for autistic adults paired with autistic compared to typically developing partners. *Autism: The International Journal of Research and Practice 24*, 5, 1067–1080.

Mulchay, W. (2012) *Zach Apologizes.* Minneapolis, MN: Free Spirit Publishing.

Mulchay, W. (2012) *Zach Gets Frustrated.* Minneapolis, MN: Free Spirit Publishing.

Mulchay, W. (2016) *Zach Makes Mistakes.* Minneapolis, MN: Free Spirit Publishing.

Mulchay, W. (2017) *Zach Hangs in There.* Minneapolis, MN: Free Spirit Publishing.

Murphy, K. (2023) *A Guide to Neurodiversity in the Early Years.* London: Anna Freud Centre.

Murray, D., Lesser, M., Lawson, W. (2005) Attention, monotropism and the diagnostic criteria for autism. *Autism 9*, 2, 139–156.

Murray, F. (2018) Me and monotropism: A unified theory of autism. *The Psychologist.* Accessed on 17 April 2025 at www.bps.org.uk/psychologist/me-and-monotropism-unified-theory-autism

Needler, M., Southam, P. (2015) *Minecraft: Construction Handbook (Updated Edition): An Official Mojang Book.* New York: Scholastic Inc.

Ratcliffe, B., Wong, M., Dossetor, D., Hayes, S. (2014) Teaching social-emotional skills to school-aged children with Autism Spectrum Disorder:

A treatment versus control trial in 41 mainstream schools. *Research in Autism Spectrum Disorders 8*, 12, 1722–1733.

Reichow, B., Steiner, A.M., Volkmar, F. (2012) Social skills groups for people aged 6 to 21 with autism spectrum disorders (ASD). *Cochrane Database of Systematic Reviews*, 7.

Roberts, J. (2020) "Training" Social Skills is Dehumanizing (Part 1). Therapist Neurodiversity Collective. Accessed on 17 April 2025 at https://therapistndc.org/training-social-skills-is-dehumanizing-part-1

Roberts, J. (2020) Why perspective-taking and neurodiversity acceptance? (Part 2 of "Training" Social Skills is Dehumanizing: The One with the Therapy Goals). Accessed on 17 April 2025 at https://therapistndc.org/why-teach-perspective-taking-neurodiversity-acceptance

Shapiro, L.E. (2004) *101 Ways to Teach Children Social Skills: A Ready-to-Use Reproducible Activity Book.* Bohemia, NY: Bureau for At-Risk Youth.

Smith Myles, B., Southwick, J. (2005) *Asperger Syndrome and Difficult Moments: Practical Solutions for Tantrums, Rage, and Meltdowns (Second Edition).* Shawnee, KS: Autism Asperger Publishing Co.

Smith, B. (2015) *If Winning Isn't Everything, Why Do I Hate to Lose?* Boys Town, NE: Boys Town Press.

Smith, B. (2016) *My Day Is Ruined!* Boys Town, NE: Boys Town Press.

Smith, B. (2016) *What Were You Thinking!* Boys Town, NE: Boys Town Press.

Smith, B. (2017) *Of Course It's a Big Deal!* Boys Town, NE: Boys Town Press.

Walker, S., Berthelsen, D.C. (2007) The social participation of young children with developmental disabilities in inclusive early childhood programs. *Electronic Journal for Inclusive Education* 2, 2.

Whelton, E. (2020) *Konfident Kidz – Konnect Book 1.* Bandon, Ireland: Ausome Training.

Whelton, E. (2020) *Konfident Kidz – Konnect Book 2.* Bandon, Ireland: Ausome Training.

Whelton, E. (2020) *Konfident Kidz – Konnect Book 3.* Bandon, Ireland: Ausome Training.

Williams, C., Wright, B. (2004) *How to Live with Autism and Asperger Syndrome: Practical Strategies for Parents and Professionals.* London: Jessica Kingsley Publishers.

Wong, C., Odom, S.L., Hume, K.A., Cox, A.W. *et al.* (2015) Evidence-based practices for children, youth, and young adults with autism spectrum disorder: A comprehensive review. *Journal of Autism and Developmental Disorders* 45, 7, 1951–1966.